GASTRONO GEEK ANIME

40 RECIPES INSPIRED BY THE GREATEST ANIME

THIBAUD VILLANOVA

GASTRONO GEEK ANIME

40 RECIPES INSPIRED BY THE GREATEST ANIME

PHOTOGRAPHY
Nicolas **LOBBESTAËL**

PHOTO STYLING
Mehdiya **KERAIRIA**

ILLUSTRATIONS
Bérengère **DEMONCY**

TITAN
BOOKS

Welcome to the first cookbook that truly gives you what I like to call the Shonen Spirit! If you know me, you know you're holding the fruit of months of hard work recreating recipes from the most iconic anime of recent years, with the utmost respect for the work, creators, and fans.

For those of you who do not know me, this book is my seventeenth cookbook dedicated to popular culture. Since 2014, my quest to make cooking accessible to all has taken me around the world and allowed me to meet many people – chefs, writers, creators, producers, – who have enabled me to forge an enormous melting pot in which to combine the greatest references and recipes of pop culture and the otaku world.

This book is therefore dedicated to the most legendary anime that have been recommended by all you weebs. In these recipes, you will find an eclectic mix of anime references, from masterpieces *Cowboy Bebop* or *Fruits Basket* for the veterans among you, to newer hits. Discover 30 exclusive recipes such as the beef bento from the *Mugen Train* and udon with yam from *Demon Slayer*, Saitama's sukiyaki, a complete course on Ichiraku ramen to delight your ninja taste buds, as well as typical Japanese recipes inspired by *Assassination Classroom*, *Aggretsuko*, *Dorohedoro*, *Kuroko's Basketball*, *One Piece*, *Jujutsu Kaisen*, *Tokyo Revengers*, etc.

I wanted this book to be a gourmet tribute to all anime in which gastronomy, and Japanese cuisine in particular, plays such an important role. You can therefore find in this book not only introductions to classic anime, but also background information on the culinary techniques and flavors of the Land of the Rising Sun. My goal is to explain the vocabulary and most commonly used cooking techniques to enable you to reproduce these recipes with perfect ease.

It was a real pleasure to undertake this gourmet quest into the heart of the anime universe. I sincerely hope you will enjoy it as much as I have!

Itadakimasu!

Thibaud Villanova
Gastronogeek

Contents

DESSERTS & DRINKS

TIPS

STREET

FOOD

FRUITS BASKET

LEVEL ✦
For 4 people
Preparation time: 10 min
Cooking time: 25 min
Rest time: 10 min

CANNIBAL ONIGIRI

VINEGAR RICE BALLS STUFFED WITH LEEKS AND BARLEY MISO BUTTER

INGREDIENTS

FOR THE STUFFING
1 small leek
2 tbsp. (25 g) butter
1 tbsp. (10 g) barley miso
1 tbsp. soy sauce

FOR THE RICE
3 cups (400 g) japonica or arborio rice
6 tbsp. and 2 tsp. (100 ml) rice vinegar
3 tbsp. (45 g) caster sugar
1 tsp. (5 g) salt
1 dried nori leaf

Tohru might say that you are like a rice dumpling: each person, like each dumpling, contains a filling, their unique qualities. Except that you don't see yours, it is buried too deep inside you. But don't worry! Tohru is certain that your qualities are there, and she sees them perfectly well.

✤ Rinse the rice several times until the water runs clear. Pour it into a saucepan with 2 cups (500 ml) of water and bring to a boil. Cook for 12 minutes on a very low heat, then let the rice rest, covered and off the heat, for 10 minutes.

✤ Meanwhile, pour the vinegar, sugar, and salt into a saucepan. Melt over low heat but do not bring to the boil. Set aside.

✤ Collect the rice and place it in a large bowl. Pour the vinegar mixture over it and mix well with a wooden spatula, so as not to crush the rice grains. Using a fan, let the rice cool while you stir in the vinegar. The onigiri rice is now ready. Keep it under a damp cloth while you make the filling.

✤ Rinse and finely chop the leek. Set it aside for a few moments. Now it's time to make the miso butter: put the butter in a bowl and add the miso. Use a flexible spatula to work the butter and incorporate the miso. Put the miso butter in a pan and melt it over medium heat. Add the leek and fry for 2 minutes before adding the soy sauce. Mix well and cover, then keep cooking on low heat for 10 minutes. Once the butter and soy sauce have been fully absorbed by the leeks, remove them from the heat.

✤ Now shape the onigiri: take a good quantity of rice in the palm of your hand. In the middle of the rice, add 1 tbsp. of leek filling. Close it over with a little rice and press lightly with your hands to mold the onigiri. Feel free to use cat-shaped molds to give a kawaii shape to your onigiri. Cut strips or shapes out of the dried nori leaf and place them on the onigiri. Now all that is left to do is eat them!

DOROHEDORO

LEVEL ✦
For 16 gyozas
Preparation time: 30 min
Cooking time: 10 min

SPECIAL NIKAIDO

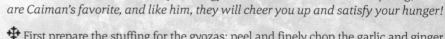

MEAT AND SHISO GYOZAS

INGREDIENTS

16 shiso leaves
16 disks of gyozas dough
Vegetable oil

FOR THE STUFFING
½ lb. and 2 ounces (300 g) ground
meat (pork preferred,
or beef or poultry)
1 clove of garlic
0.8-inch (2 cm) ginger
2 spring onions
2 large button mushrooms or shiitakes
4 shiso leaves
4 tsp. (20ml) cooking sake
3 tbsp. and 1 tsp. (50 ml) soy sauce
Salt

Here's how to make Nikaido's famous gyozas! With a meat and shiso filling, these are Caiman's favorite, and like him, they will cheer you up and satisfy your hunger!

✠ First prepare the stuffing for the gyozas: peel and finely chop the garlic and ginger. Finely chop the spring onions. Peel and chop the mushrooms. Chop the shiso leaves. Put all the ingredients in a bowl. Then add the meat. Season with salt, sake, and soy sauce. Mix everything thoroughly for 5 minutes until all ingredients are perfectly incorporated. Your stuffing is ready, put it aside in the refrigerator for a few moments.

✠ Rinse and gently dry the shiso leaves. Remove the stems and central stalk.

✠ Now fill the discs of gyoza dough: lightly flour your work surface and place down 1 disc of dough. Moisten the edges with a little water using a brush or the tip of your index finger. In the center of the disk, place 1 shiso leaf and then, in the centre of that, place 1 teaspoon full of stuffing. Fold the disk over the filling and press it tightly together. Seal the gyozas well to prevent them from opening during cooking. Repeat until all ingredients are used up.

✠ Now it's time to cook: drizzle a good amount of vegetable oil into a pan and heat over medium heat. Place the raw gyozas in the pan and grill them on one side for 1 ½ to 2 minutes until golden brown. Add 2 to 3 tbsp. of water and cover. Continue cooking for 2 minutes before uncovering. Finish by letting the gyozas cook for 1 more minute. The idea is that the base of the gyozas should be golden brown and crispy while the rest of the dumpling should be soft.

✠ Cover the pan with a plate and gently flip the gyozas directly onto the plate. Serve hot with chili sauce to enjoy!

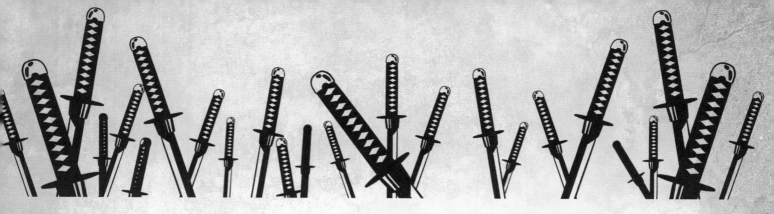

SAMURAI CHAMPLOO

LEVEL ✦
For 16 skewers
Preparation time: 15 min
Cooking time: 15 min

JIN'S DANGO
MITARASHI DANGO AND SAUCE

INGREDIENTS

FOR THE DANGO
½ lb. (250 g) firm tofu
1 cup and 5 tbsp. (160 g)
mochiko flour
2 tbsp. vegetable oil

FOR THE SWEET SAUCE
½ cup and 5 tbsp. (200 ml) soy sauce
1 cup (200 g) brown sugar
6 tbsp. and 2 tsp. (100 ml) water
2 tbsp. (20 g) potato starch

EQUIPMENT

16 skewers

Jin likes nothing more than a melting, sticky dango covered in syrupy sauce!

✤ First prepare the dango dough: place the tofu in a bowl and, using your hands, mash or puree. Mix in the mochiko flour and knead until the mixture is smooth and almost silky.

✤ Shape the dango balls by taking a small amount of dough with your fingertips and rolling them in the palm of your hands. Continue until the dough is used up.

✤ Now it's time to cook the dango. Prepare a large volume of ice water. Then, bring a large volume of water to a boil and plunge in the raw dango for 5 minutes, until they rise to the surface of the boiling water. Remove the cooked dango with a skimmer and immediately plunge them into ice water to stop the cooking process and firm them up.

✤ Drain and skewer the dango, then grill them: in a large frying pan, pour 2 tbsp. of vegetable oil and heat over medium heat. Grill the skewers for 1 minute on each side, then remove them.

✤ Finish by preparing the sauce: pour all the ingredients into the pan over low heat and mix until smooth. Heat the resulting sauce, stirring constantly, until it thickens. Then pour it into a measuring glass so that you can dip the dango skewers into it. Serve immediately!

ASSASSINATION CLASSROOM

LEVEL ✦ ✦
For 4 people
Preparation time: 15 min
Cooking time: 5 min

SENSEI'S TAKOYAKI
GRILLED OCTOPUS DOUGH BALLS

INGREDIENTS

2 pre-cooked octopus tentacles
10 sprigs of chives
¼ cup (40 g) pickled ginger
6 tbsp. and 2 tsp. (100 ml) Japanese mayonnaise (see Tips page 114)
6 tbsp. and 2 tsp. (100 ml) of takoyaki sauce
4 tbsp. Katsuobushi nori powder

FOR THE TAKOYAKI DOUGH

1 cup and 8 tbsp. (200 g) flour
2 whole eggs
1 ⅞ cups (450 ml) dried bonito dashi or vegetable broth (see Tips on pages 110 and 113)
1 tbsp. soy sauce
Vegetable oil

EQUIPMENT

Takoyaki plate
Takoyaki pick or wooden skewer

Finding a dead octopus on his desk, stabbed by a combat knife, is not enough to intimidate Koro-sensei. Nothing could motivate him more to cook hot takoyaki, grilled with the flame of a ballistic missile!

✤ First prepare the octopus: cut it into small regular-sized cubes. Set aside. Rinse and dry the chives, then chop them finely and set aside.

✤ Prepare the takoyaki dough: pour the flour into a bowl and break the eggs. Whisk vigorously then add the broth and soy sauce. Your takoyaki dough is ready, now go ahead and cook it!

✤ Heat the takoyaki pan and grease each mold well. Once the molds are hot, fill them with takoyaki dough. Place a dice of octopus and a pinch of chives in each mold. When the edges of the dough begin to lift slightly from the molds, use a takoyaki skewer or a small wooden skewer to roll the dough into each mold. This is the most complicated part of the recipe, so feel free to practice. Let the dough cook again and repeat the process until you have a nice round ball. The idea is to have balls that are crispy on the outside and very soft on the inside.

✤ Once your takoyaki are done, remove them and place them in bamboo serving trays.

✤ Takoyaki is best eaten right after cooking. Brush them with takoyaki sauce and Japanese mayonnaise. Sprinkle them with green nori powder and place a few pinches of katsuobushi on top. Enjoy!

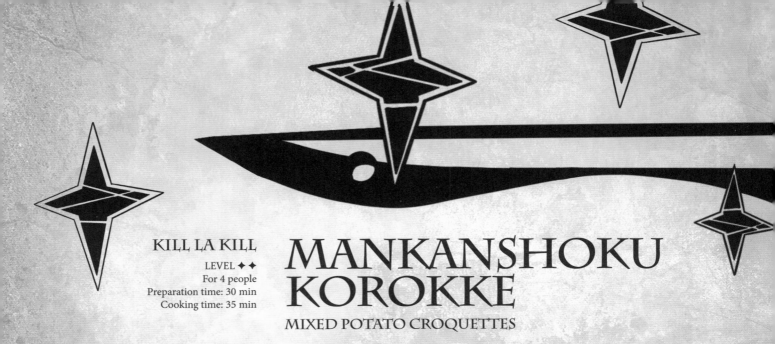

KILL LA KILL

LEVEL ✦ ✦
For 4 people
Preparation time: 30 min
Cooking time: 35 min

MANKANSHOKU KOROKKE
MIXED POTATO CROQUETTES

INGREDIENTS

FOR THE KOROKKE
6 large potatoes, mashed
1 tbsp. and ½ tsp. (20 g) coarse salt
6 cups and 4 tbsp. (1.5 l) frying oil

FOR THE KOROKKE GARNISH
1 spring onion
½ bunch of flat-leaf parsley
3 button mushrooms
½ can of sardines in olive oil
1 clove of garlic
4 shrimps
Soy sauce
1 ¾ ounces (50 g)
pre-cooked edamame
Olive oil

FOR THE BREADCRUMBS
2 eggs
8 tbsp. (80 g) potato starch or flour
1 cup and 5 tbsp. (140 g)
panko breadcrumbs
Salt

The korokke, or croquettes, are the perfect way for Mama Mankanshoku to finish the leftovers in the fridge and to make a gourmet meal for everyone to share...

✢ Prepare the potatoes: rinse and scrub them under water before placing them in a pot. Cover with 2 liters of cold water, add the coarse salt, and bring to the boil. Continue cooking for 20 minutes, until the potatoes are soft in the middle.

✢ In the meantime, prepare the ingredients for the croquettes. Finely chop the spring onion and parsley. Peel and coarsely chop the mushrooms. Remove the backbones from the sardines and crush them in a bowl.

✢ Prepare the garlic shrimp: peel, de-seed, and chop the garlic. Pour 1 tbsp. of olive oil into a frying pan and heat over medium heat. Add the garlic and half of the chopped parsley. Fry until the garlic begins to brown, or for about 1.5 minutes. Add the shrimp and deglaze with soy sauce. Fry for 1 min on each side until they have changed color completely. Remove from the heat, peel, and coarsely chop the shrimp. Put them aside in a bowl with their cooking juices.

✢ Drain the potatoes and peel them with a paring knife. You can run them under cold water for a few moments so you can handle them without burning yourself. Then mash the potatoes with a potato masher or with a fork to make a coarse purée. Stir in the spring onion and parsley. Separate the mashed potatoes into 3 different bowls to make 3 different types of croquettes.

✢ In the first bowl, mix in the crushed sardines. In the second bowl, mix in the shrimp with garlic and soy sauce. In the last bowl, mix in the mushrooms and edamame.

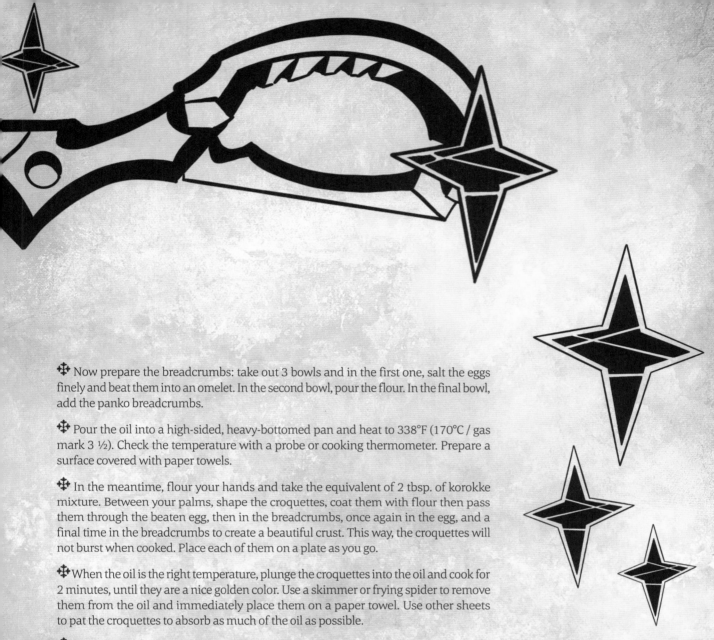

✤ Now prepare the breadcrumbs: take out 3 bowls and in the first one, salt the eggs finely and beat them into an omelet. In the second bowl, pour the flour. In the final bowl, add the panko breadcrumbs.

✤ Pour the oil into a high-sided, heavy-bottomed pan and heat to 338°F (170°C / gas mark 3 ½). Check the temperature with a probe or cooking thermometer. Prepare a surface covered with paper towels.

✤ In the meantime, flour your hands and take the equivalent of 2 tbsp. of korokke mixture. Between your palms, shape the croquettes, coat them with flour then pass them through the beaten egg, then in the breadcrumbs, once again in the egg, and a final time in the breadcrumbs to create a beautiful crust. This way, the croquettes will not burst when cooked. Place each of them on a plate as you go.

✤ When the oil is the right temperature, plunge the croquettes into the oil and cook for 2 minutes, until they are a nice golden color. Use a skimmer or frying spider to remove them from the oil and immediately place them on a paper towel. Use other sheets to pat the croquettes to absorb as much of the oil as possible.

✤ Serve your delicious korokke with fresh, crisp salad leaves.
You can also serve them with hot sauce!

GTO

LEVEL ✦
Serves 4 (16 dumplings)
Preparation time: 20 min
Cooking time: 10 min

CURSED DUMPLING WITH HUMAN FLESH

REVISITED SIU MAI DUMPLINGS

Do you know the story of the cursed dumpling? The dumpling with human flesh that suddenly disappears as soon as you open the box in which they are stored? No? Then let me tell you the recipe, and Onizuka will tell you the story!

✤ First prepare the stuffing: peel and chop the onion and garlic. Peel the ginger and chop it finely. Wash, rinse, and chop the chives. Rinse and drain the bamboo shoots and coarsely chop them. Chop the shrimp. Place all ingredients in a bowl. Add the minced meat, salt, pepper, soy sauce, black sesame oil, rice wine, and potato starch. Mix thoroughly for several minutes until the mixture is smooth and fragrant. Set aside.

✤ Bring a large pot of salted water to a boil and boil the peas for 3 minutes. Immediately soak them in a bowl of cold water and drain. Set aside.

✤ Bring a large volume of water to a boil and place a steamer basket on top: coat it with a little olive oil so that the dumplings do not stick to the pan.

✤ Now fill the dumpling wrappers with the stuffing: place 1 wrapper on the work surface and moisten it slightly. In the center, place 1 heaped teaspoon of filling. Fold the sheet all around the stuffing and tighten it well. Repeat the process until all ingredients are used up. Place the dumpling in the steamer basket, cover it, and cook for 10 minutes.

Enjoy hot with a little black vinegar and 1 pea on top.

INGREDIENTS

16 dumpling wrappers
1 onion
2 cloves of garlic
⅓ inch (1 cm) of fresh ginger
½ bunch of chives
2 ounces (60 g) canned bamboo shoots
7 ounces (200 g) peeled prawns
3 ½ ounces (100 g) ground pork, beef, or poultry
1 tsp. (5 g) salt
1 tbsp. (5 g) pepper
1 tbsp. soy sauce
1 tsp. black sesame oil
1 tbsp. shaoxing rice wine
2 tbsp. (20 g) potato starch
16 garden peas
Olive oil
Black vinegar for the dressing

EQUIPMENT

Steamer basket

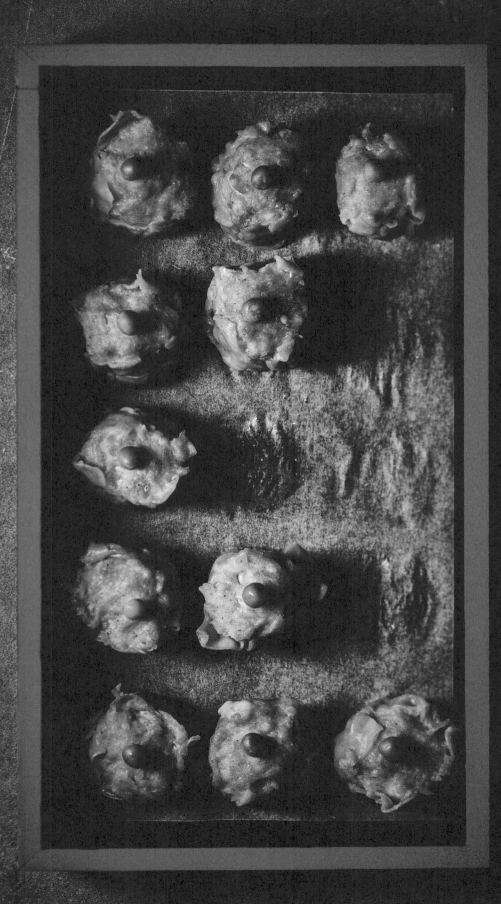

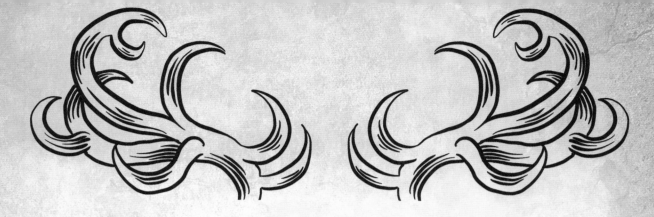

BEASTARS

LEVEL ✦
For 4 people
Preparation time: 15 min
Cooking time: 7 min

WEDNESDAY EGG SANDO

SCRAMBLED EGG SANDWICHES

INGREDIENTS

8 slices of bread
8 eggs
2 tbsp. homemade Japanese mayonnaise (see Tips on page 114)
1 pinch of sugar
Salt, pepper

Not sure Legoshi ever knew how seriously Legom took her job as a laying hen: laying high-quality eggs was more than a job for her, it was her passion! That's why these egg sandwiches are so good, they're made with eggs that are full of love!

✤ Start by cooking the eggs: bring a pot of water to a boil and boil the eggs for 7 minutes. Prepare a large volume of ice water and immerse the eggs, once they have been boiling for 7 minutes.

✤ Peel the eggs while in the water and then place them in a mixing bowl.

✤ Mash them with a fork or a potato masher: the idea is to crush the eggs and mix the white with the yolk. Add the homemade Japanese mayonnaise, a good pinch of salt, and the sugar. Mix well. Your egg filling is ready!

✤ To match the sandwiches from the anime, cut the crust off the slices of bread with a knife. Cover 4 slices of bread evenly with egg filling. Cover them with the remaining 4 slices of bread and press gently to make the sandwiches. Cut them in half and arrange them on a plate, ready to serve. Itadakimasu!

CRAZY PIZZA

TOMATO, CHEESE, SMOKED BACON, AND GREEN ASPARAGUS PIZZA

SILVER SPOON

LEVEL ✦ ✦
For 4 people
Preparation time: 15 min
Rest time: 1 h to 12 h
Cooking time: 15 min
+ 1 min 30 in a pizza oven
or 15 min in a traditional oven

INGREDIENTS

FOR THE PIZZA DOUGH

½ tsp. (3 g) yeast or 1 packet
of baking powder
6 tbsp. (150 g) flour type T45 or 00
6 tbsp. (85 ml) water at room
temperature
1 tsp. (4 g) olive oil
A pinch (4 g) of salt
Semolina or flour
(to work the dough)

FOR THE GARNISH

8 organic cherry
or datterini tomatoes
1 shallot
1 clove of garlic
1 large mushroom
2 green asparagus
2 slices of smoked bacon
3 ounces (80 g) of cheese
(mozzarella, raclette or Abondance)
1 pinch of sugar
Olive oil
Salt, pepper

EQUIPMENT

Food processor
Hand blender

This is typically the kind of dish you can make with that old oven: a pizza with crispy dough, a good tomato sauce, and above extra-melted cheese… That oven won't go to waste any longer!

✤ 1 hour before or the day before, start preparing the pizza dough: if you are using baking powder, empty the packet into a small bowl, fill the packet with warm water, and pour it over the yeast. Mix well and let it settle for 5 minutes.

✤ Pour all the ingredients for the dough, including the yeast, into the bowl of a food processor or a mixing bowl. Knead on first speed for 2 minutes to solidify the dough and then knead 4-5 minutes faster.

✤ If you are kneading by hand, solidify the dough by kneading in the bowl. Flour your work surface and place down your dough. Knead it firmly by hand for 10 to 15 minutes until you have a nice smooth dough.

✤ When the dough is smooth and nicely formed, place it in a bowl, cover with a cloth, and let it rest in a warm environment (near a radiator, in a high place, etc.). If you have prepared your dough the day before, wrap it in clingfilm and place it in the refrigerator. The dough will grow slowly but surely over time.

✤ Preheat your traditional oven, equipped with an oven stone, to 428°F (220°C / gas mark 7), or 752°F (400°C) if you have a pizza oven.

✤ Now prepare the homemade tomato sauce and vegetables: rinse and quarter the tomatoes. Peel and chop the shallot. Peel, degerm, and mince the garlic clove. Clean the mushroom with a lightly moistened paper towel. Slice the mushroom. Peel the asparagus and remove the stalks. Cut the slices of smoked bacon in four parts.

✤ Prepare a large bowl of ice water. Bring a large volume of salted water to a boil and boil the asparagus into it for 2 minutes. Immediately plunge them in the ice water and drain. Cut them into 4 strips.

✤ Now it's time to cook: drizzle olive oil into a saucepan and heat over medium heat. Add the shallot, garlic, and smoked bacon and sauté for a few moments before adding the chopped tomatoes. Season with salt and pepper and add the sugar. Melt the tomatoes for 10-12 minutes. Remove the slices of bacon and, using a hand blender, blend the contents of the pan. The sauce is ready!

✤ Next prepare the pizza dough: roll out the dough on your work surface, covered with a little flour or semolina. Spread the sauce on top of the dough, then add the pine nuts, the smoked bacon, and the asparagus. Finally, place the slices of cheese on top and bake for 1.5 minutes in a pizza oven or 15 minutes in a conventional oven.

BLACK BUTLER

LEVEL ✦ ✦
For 4 people
Preparation time: 30 min
Rest time: 1 h
Cooking time: 2 h 10

SEBASTIAN'S DEMONIC CURRY

FRIED BREAD STUFFED WITH JAPANESE CURRY

INGREDIENTS

14 ounces (400 g) of beef cheek
Olive oil
Sesame oil
1 tbsp. flour
2 tsp. garam masala
6 ⅓ cups (1,5 l) chicken
or vegetable stock (see Tips
on pages 112 and 113)
3 tbsp. homemade curry powder
(see recipe page 60) or 4 tbsp
ready-made curry powder
1 square of dark chocolate
Salt, pepper

FOR THE JAPANESE CURRY
2 onions
2 heads of garlic
1/3 inch (1 cm) of fresh ginger
2 carrots
1 celery stalk

FOR THE BREAD DOUGH
2 packets of baking powder
3 cups (360 g) flour
2 pinches of salt
⅔ cup (150 ml) warm milk
2 tbsp. vegetable oil

FOR THE BREADCRUMBS
½ cup and 5 tbsp. (100 g) flour
1 cup (100 g) panko breadcrumbs
2 eggs, beaten
4 cups (1 l) frying oil

This recipe will allow you to cook a devilish curry and win any cooking contest. OK, my Lord!

✤ Start by preparing the Japanese curry. Peel and finely chop the onions, garlic, and ginger. Peel the carrots and cut them into 5 mm cubes. Do the same with the celery stalk.

✤ Move on to the meat: cut the beef cheek into small cubes and lightly salt and pepper them. Your ingredients are ready to be cooked!

✤ Pour a large drizzle of olive oil and sesame oil into a cast iron casserole dish and heat over medium heat. Once the oil is hot, add the onions, carrots, and celery and sauté for 4 minutes before adding the garlic and ginger.

✤ Continue to color the filling without burning it and place the beef cheek pieces on top. Brown them on all sides before sprinkling them finely with flour and garam masala. Deglaze with the broth. Mix all ingredients well. Lower the heat, cover, and simmer on a low heat for 2 hours.

✤ When the cooking time is over, pour the broth into a large saucepan, using a cheesecloth to strain the mixture and separate the broth from the meat.

✤ Stir the curry powder into the meat broth to make a thick, fragrant sauce. Finally, roughly chop the dark chocolate and stir it into the sauce. Add the meat and vegetables to the sauce and mix well. Your curry is ready, keep it covered and on a very low heat.

✤ While the meat is cooking, prepare the bread dough. Start by activating the yeast by pouring it into 50 ml of warm water (between 95 and 104°F (35 and 40 °C)). Let it rest and thicken for 3 minutes. Pour the flour and salt into the bowl of your food processor. Mix well, then add the warm milk, the glass of yeast, and the vegetable oil. Knead with a dough hook at medium speed for 2 minutes.

✤ Flour your work surface and then, using a flexible spatula, collect the mixture obtained and place it on the flour. Knead for a few moments until you have a nice ball of stretchy dough. Place it in a bowl and cover with a slightly damp cloth. Let the dough rest and grow for 1 hour.

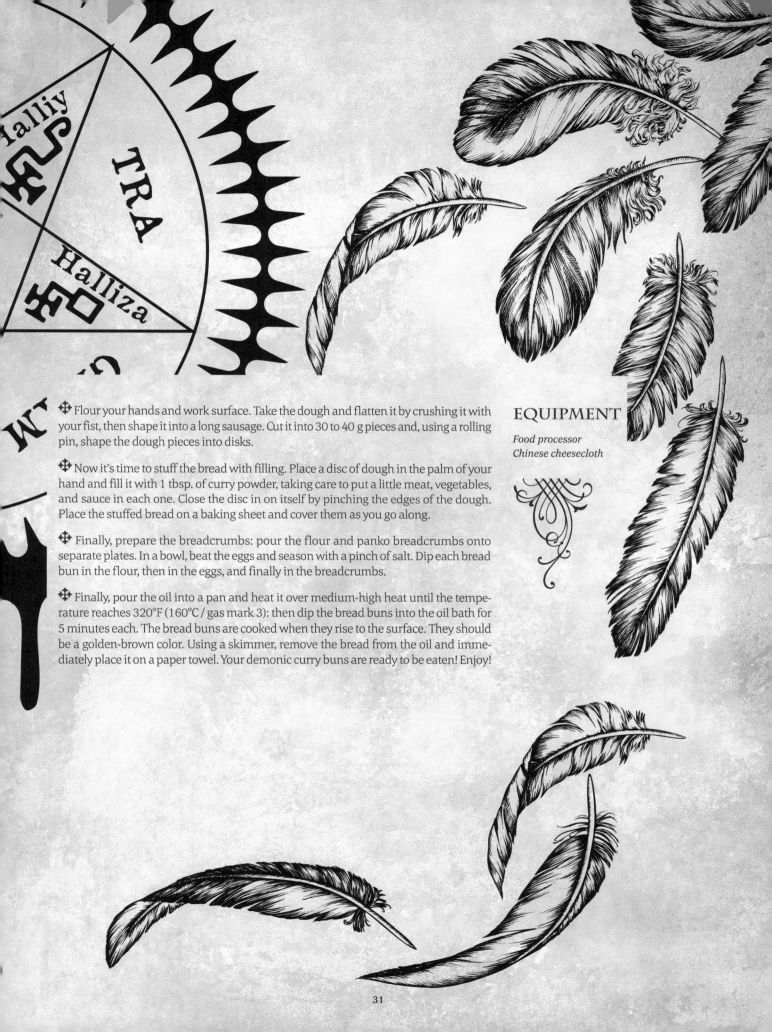

✠ Flour your hands and work surface. Take the dough and flatten it by crushing it with your fist, then shape it into a long sausage. Cut it into 30 to 40 g pieces and, using a rolling pin, shape the dough pieces into disks.

✠ Now it's time to stuff the bread with filling. Place a disc of dough in the palm of your hand and fill it with 1 tbsp. of curry powder, taking care to put a little meat, vegetables, and sauce in each one. Close the disc in on itself by pinching the edges of the dough. Place the stuffed bread on a baking sheet and cover them as you go along.

✠ Finally, prepare the breadcrumbs: pour the flour and panko breadcrumbs onto separate plates. In a bowl, beat the eggs and season with a pinch of salt. Dip each bread bun in the flour, then in the eggs, and finally in the breadcrumbs.

✠ Finally, pour the oil into a pan and heat it over medium-high heat until the temperature reaches 320°F (160°C / gas mark 3): then dip the bread buns into the oil bath for 5 minutes each. The bread buns are cooked when they rise to the surface. They should be a golden-brown color. Using a skimmer, remove the bread from the oil and immediately place it on a paper towel. Your demonic curry buns are ready to be eaten! Enjoy!

EQUIPMENT

Food processor
Chinese cheesecloth

KARAAGE FROM SUMIRE STREET

MARINATED AND FRIED CHICKEN BITES, WRAPS, FINE HERBS

FOOD WARS!

LEVEL ✦
For 4 people
Preparation time: 30 min
Resting time: 1 to 12 hours
in the refrigerator
Cooking time: 20 min

INGREDIENTS

2 little gem lettuces
4 shiso leaves or ½ bunch
of fresh mint

FOR THE MEAT
½ cup and 5 tbsp. (200 ml)
of soy sauce
6 tbsp. and 2 tsp. (100 ml) mirin
or rice vinegar
3 tbsp. and 1 tsp. (50 ml) of sake
1 tsp. sesame oil
1 tbsp. liquid honey
1 clove of garlic
1 tsp. pepper
1 tsp. chili purée
4 boneless chicken legs
1 cup (100 g) potato starch
8 cups (2 l) frying oil
Salt

FOR THE FOR THE WRAPS
1 cup and 12 tbsp. (200 g) rice flour
2 eggs
½ cup and 5 tbsp. (200 ml) milk
2 tbsp. sunflower oil
1 good pinch of salt

There is no way you are going to let this chain restaurant tarnish the life and businesses of Sumire Street. You need to find a way to create crispy, perfectly cooked karaage that will crush the competition and revive your neighborhood. Why not enjoy them in wraps?

✤ First prepare the marinade for the chicken: pour the soy sauce, mirin, sake, sesame oil, and honey into a bowl. Mix well. Peel and chop the garlic, then add it to the marinade, along with the pepper and chili paste. Cut the chicken thighs into pieces 2 to 3 cm wide. Lightly salt them and place them in the marinade. Dip them well into the mixture and place the chicken in the refrigerator for at least 1 hour.

✤ Meanwhile, prepare the rice wraps that will accompany the karaage. Pour the flour into a bowl and make a well in the center. Break the eggs into the well and whisk until the mixture thickens. While mixing, add the milk. Add the oil and salt.

✤ Heat a pancake pan over medium heat and grease it with a drop of oil. Once the oil is hot, pour in a small ladleful of wrap batter and cook until the edges come away from the pan. Turn it over and cook for another 30 seconds. Place the resulting wrap on a plate, cover it, and continue the process until you have used up all the batter.

✤ Now it's time to prepare the karaage! Pour the potato starch onto a plate. Take the chicken pieces out of the bowl and place them in the potato starch, coating them well. Set them aside for a few moments.

✤ Pour the marinade into a small saucepan and bring it to a boil. Reduce it for 5 minutes before removing it to a bowl. You can use it as a sauce for your karaage.

✤ Pour the frying oil into a high-sided pan and heat it to 320°F (160°C / gas mark 3). Prepare a dish lined with paper towels. Once the oil is hot, dip the chicken pieces in it and fry them for 5 minutes before placing them on the paper towel. Your karaage is ready, now move on to preparing the wraps.

To make the wraps: take 1 wrap, coat it with the reduced marinade, place some little gem lettuce leaves and mint leaves on top, then add the karaage. Roll up the patty and enjoy.

SWORD ART
ONLINE

LEVEL ✦ ✦
For 2 sandwiches
Preparation time: 20 min
Rest time: 1 h 30
Cooking time: 15 min

ASUNA'S DELICIOUS SANDWICH

BAGUETTE WITH MARINATED STEAK, SPINACH, AND SPICY MAYONNAISE

INGREDIENTS

3 tbsp. of soy sauce
2 tbsp. of rice vinegar
1 tsp. oyster sauce
1 clove of garlic
1 pinch of ground black pepper
10 ounces (300 g) rib-eye steak
2 whole eggs
1 egg yolk
1 tsp. mustard
Salt
Sriracha sauce
2 tbsp. (30 ml) sunflower oil
10 fresh spinach leaves
1 baguette
Some edible flowers

With a sandwich like this, it's easy to see why Asuna is in charge of the Brotherhood of Knights!

✠ Start by preparing the marinade for the meat: in a freezer bag, pour the soy sauce, rice vinegar, and oyster sauce. Peel the garlic and chop it finely. Add it to the mixture with the black pepper. Finally, place the meat in the bag, close it tightly, and mix it all together.

✠ Let the meat marinate for 1 hour and a half in the refrigerator (you can also cook it right away, but it will be less tasty). Use this time to prepare the hard-boiled eggs and spicy mayonnaise.

✠ Bring a pot of water to a boil and immerse the eggs in it. Keep boiling and cook for 10 minutes. Remove the eggs from the pan, run them under cold water, and peel them. They are now ready.

✠ Now move onto the spicy mayonnaise. The secret to making mayonnaise easily is that all of the ingredients should be at room temperature.

✠ In a mixing bowl, pour the egg yolk, add the mustard, 1 pinch of salt, and 1 half teaspoon of sriracha sauce. Use a whisk to mix all the ingredients together. Then drizzle in the sunflower oil evenly, while whisking, to make the mayonnaise rise. Set it aside in a cool place and move onto cooking the meat.

✠ Put 1 tbsp. of sunflower oil in a frying pan over medium-high heat. Once the oil is hot, place the meat in the pan and cook for 1 minute on each side so that a crust forms. Lower the heat and cook for another 4 minutes. Remove the meat to a paper towel and let it rest for 5 minutes.

✠ Rinse, drain, and dry the spinach leaves well. Now it's time to put together the sandwich. Cut the baguette in half and then cut each piece lengthwise. Coat each side with spicy mayonnaise. Place a few spinach leaves on the bottom side. Cut the eggs into strips and place them on the spinach leaves. Slice the meat into two equal pieces and place them on top of the egg strips. Finish by placing some edible flowers and putting the other part of the bread on top.

✠ Beware, this sandwich does not keep long; it is best eaten immediately! You'll find that it's so good that it would bring in a fortune at an auction…

LEVEL ✦
For 3 people
Preparation time: 15 min
Cooking time: 12 min

COMFORT EGGS

FRIED POACHED EGGS, MISO, CHILI, DASHI

INGREDIENTS

3 large fresh organic eggs
1 tbsp. and 1 tsp. (20 ml) white vinegar
8 cups (2 l) of water

FOR THE BREADCRUMBS
3 eggs
*4 cups (1 l) vegetable oil
(sunflower or grape seed)*
½ cup and 5 tbsp. (100 g) of flour
1 cup (100 g) panko breadcrumbs
1 tsp. miso (white, red, or classic)
1 tsp. yuzukosho or chili paste
½ bag of dashi powder

There's nothing like a good fried egg with a runny heart to fill your belly – but not too much – just after a nice hot bath with your friends...

✤ Start by poaching the eggs: pour the vinegar and water into a large saucepan and bring it to a boil. Prepare a large volume of ice water in a bowl. Break the first egg into a bowl. With a spoon, create a whirlpool in the boiling water and, in the center of the whirlpool, quickly dunk the egg. The white will automatically close over the yolk and the egg will fall to the bottom of the pan. After 3 minutes, remove the egg with a skimmer and carefully place it in the ice water. Repeat the process with the other 2 eggs. Put them aside in the ice water.

✤ Now move onto preparing the breadcrumbs: pour the oil into a pan and prepare a plate covered with paper towels. Heat the oil to 338°F (170°C / gas mark 3 ½). Pour the flour into a plate or a large bowl and do the same with the panko breadcrumbs. Break the eggs into 3 separate bowls and beat vigorously. In the first bowl, add the miso. In the second bowl, add the yuzukosho or chili paste and mix well. In the last bowl, add the dashi powder.

✤ Remove the eggs from the ice water and dry them gently with a paper towel. Dredge the first egg in flour, then in the miso mixture, and then in the panko breadcrumbs. Do the same with the second egg using the chili mixture and the third egg in the dashi mixture.

✤ Once the eggs are covered with breadcrumbs, dip them in the oil for 30 seconds: the idea is to brown the breadcrumbs but not overcook the egg. Remove the eggs, place on paper towels, and blot them gently. Now all you have to do is eat them!

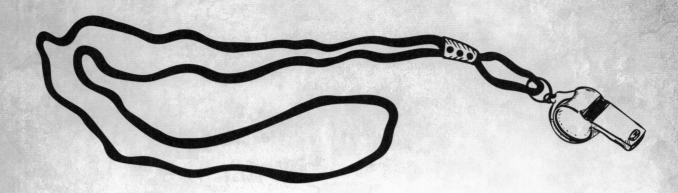

KUROKO'S BASKETBALL

LEVEL ✦
For 4 people
Preparation time: 15 min
Cooking time: 7 min

INGREDIENTS

1 ½ cup (200 g) of flour
2 eggs
1 level tsp. of salt
6 tbsp. and 2 tsp. (100 ml) of dashi
broth with dried bonito
(see Tips on page 110)
2 tbsp. soy sauce
1 tsp. sesame oil
1 tsp. chili miso
6 Napa cabbage leaves
2 green onions
8 radishes
6 button mushrooms or shiitakes
2 new carrots
Homemade okonomi sauce
(see Tips on page 114)
Homemade Japanese mayonnaise
(see Tips on page 114)
Green nori powder
Katsuobushi (dried bonito chips)
Olive oil

OKONO KAGAMI
OKONOMIYAKI WITH VEGETABLES AND SPICY MISO

There's nothing like a good, crispy, melting, sauce-filled okonomiyaki to recover from a workout and to get you ready for the inter-school tournament! Anyway, considering the amount he has eaten, Kagami knows the power of these grilled pancakes...

✤ First prepare the okonomiyaki mixture: pour the flour into a bowl, add the eggs and salt and mix well. When the mixture starts to thicken, add the dashi, soy sauce, and sesame oil. Dissolve the miso in 1 tbsp. and 1 tsp. (20 ml) of hot water and add it to the rest of the ingredients. Set aside.

✤ Prepare your vegetables: rinse and chop the cabbage and onions. Wash and finely chop the radishes. Chop the mushrooms and finely julienne the carrots.

✤ Stir the vegetables into the okonomiyaki mixture.

✤ Put a drizzle of olive oil in a frying pan and heat it over medium heat, then add the okonomiyaki mixture. Cover and cook over medium heat for 5 minutes. Turn over and toast for another 2 minutes. Remove to a serving plate and move onto the dressing.

Okonomiyaki would be nothing without its sauces and toppings. Spread a little okonomi sauce on the surface of the patty, followed by Japanese mayonnaise. Sprinkle with nori and finish with a few pinches of katsuobushi.

AGGRETSUKO

LEVEL ✦
For 4 people
Preparation time: 15 min
Cooking time: 15 min

ANAI'S YAKISOBA RAP

FRIED NOODLES AND OCTOPUS SAUSAGES

INGREDIENTS

1 clove of garlic
2 large spring onions
1 carrot
1 red bell pepper
2 Napa cabbage leaves
4 sausages (Knacki® type)
1 pork chop or 1 beef steak or 1 chicken fillet or 3 ½ ounces (100 g) tofu
4 portions of yakisoba noodles

FOR THE YAKISOBA SAUCE
4 tbsp. soy sauce
3 tbsp. oyster sauce
2 tbsp. ketchup
1 tsp. of mirin
1 tsp. brown sugar

There is a recipe for yakisoba that only Anai has mastered, a recipe that requires you to be in a certain state of mind to be completed to perfection, a recipe that may bring tears to your eyes… of happiness!

✤ Start by making the yakisoba sauce: mix all the ingredients and set aside.

✤ Move on to preparing the vegetables: peel, degerm, and chop the garlic. Peel and chop the onions. Chop the green onions. Peel the carrot and cut it into julienne strips. Seed and slice the bell pepper. Rinse and roughly chop the Napa cabbage.

✤ Now prepare the meat: cut each sausage into 3 pieces. Make several cuts at one end of each section. As they cook, the sausage ends will shrink and give the sausage a small octopus-like appearance.

✤ Slice the meat or tofu into thin strips.

✤ Bring a large volume of salted water to a boil and immerse the noodles. Cook them for a few minutes, following the instructions on the packet, then drain and rinse them quickly.

✤ All your ingredients are now ready, it's time to cook! To cook perfectly, use a plancha or a teppanyaki-type pan. You can also use a wok or a large frying pan. Pour 2 tbsp. of vegetable oil into your pan and heat over a high heat. Sauté the onion, carrot, bell pepper, garlic, and cabbage for 2 minutes, stirring constantly. Add the sausages and meat and sauté for 2 minutes. Finally, add the cooked noodles to the remaining ingredients and fry for 2 minutes to toast them. Finally, add the yakisoba sauce and mix-together all the ingredients.

Serve the yakisoba immediately! It's good to cry, isn't it? Want even more? Add 1 pinch of pickled ginger and a good pinch of katsuobushi to your noodles and then… U-MA-MI!

DISHES

LEVEL ✦
For 4 people
Preparation time: 15 min
Cooking time: 30 min

RENGOKU'S UMAI GYUBENTO

BEEF WITH ONIONS, MARINATED EGG, TOFU, AND CHILI

INGREDIENTS

FOR THE EGGS
2 eggs
½ cup and 2 tbsp. (150 ml) soy sauce
2 spring onions
Flower of salt

FOR THE BEEF AND ONIONS
14 ounces (400 g) flank steak
or beef steak
2 onions
1 inch (3 cm) fresh ginger
1 cup and 4 tbsp. (300 ml) dashi
or broth of your choice (see Tips
pages 110-113)
½ cup and 2 tbsp. (150 ml) soy sauce
6 tbsp. and 2 tsp. (100 ml) of mirin
2 tbsp. brown sugar
Neutral vegetable oil or toasted
sesame oil
Fine salt

FOR THE TOFU
7 ounces (200 g) firm tofu
1 tsp. chili paste

FOR THE DRESSING
1 cup (200 g) steamed round rice
Some shishito peppers

You don't know anyone who likes their food as much as Rengoku Kyojuro. He may be silent, solemn, and incredibly good at demon slaying, but he doesn't hesitate to show his joy when eating a well-made dish – like this beef bento devoured on board the Mugen Train!

✥ First prepare the eggs: fill a bowl with soy sauce. Boil a large volume of water and immerse the eggs in it for 6 minutes. While the eggs are cooking, prepare a large bowl of ice water. When the cooking time is over, remove the eggs and immediately plunge them into the ice water. Peel the eggs in the water so that the shells can be removed more easily. Dip the soft-boiled eggs in the soy sauce and set aside until ready to serve.

✥ Preheat your oven to 392°F (200°C / gas mark 6). Remove the roots and separate the bulbs from the stems of the spring onions. Separate the green parts of the stems from the white parts and cut the white parts in half, into strips. You can store the green parts and roots in the refrigerator, along with the onion skins, to make vegetable stock later. Chop the bulbs and reserve them for the beef onions. Place the spring onion stems on a baking sheet. Coat the stems with vegetable oil and sprinkle with fleur de sel. Bake for 10 to 12 minutes.

✥ Meanwhile, prepare the beef onions. Peel and chop the onions. Peel and chop the ginger. Prepare and slice the meat as finely as possible and salt it lightly.

✥ In a large frying pan, pour a good drizzle of vegetable oil and heat over medium heat. Sauté the chopped onions and spring onion for 2 minutes. Add the dashi, soy sauce, mirin, brown sugar, and chopped ginger. Bring to a boil and mix well before dipping the sliced beef into it. Continue cooking for 2 minutes, stirring well, until the meat is colored on all sides. Remove the beef and onions to a covered container. Let the contents of the pan reduce for another 5 minutes.

✤ Drain the tofu and cut it into large rectangular pieces. Place the tofu in the pan with the beef and onion sauce. Add the chili paste and mix well.

✤ Continue cooking for 5 minutes before moving onto dressing.

Arrange the rice on the bottom of 4 bento boxes so that you cover two-thirds of the surface of each box. Top with beef and onions. Slice the soft-boiled eggs in half and place them in the part of the boxes where there is no rice. Place the cubes of tofu in the sauce. Between the egg and the tofu, place the grilled onions. Between the tofu and the box, put the shishito peppers. Your bentos are now ready!

Note: to make this recipe vegan, replace the meat with seitan and use a vegetarian broth or dashi!

DEMON SLAYER

LEVEL ✦
For 4 people
Preparation time: 10 to 20 minutes
Cooking time: 30 min

ASAKUSA NOODLES

DASHI, UDON, YAM, AND RUNNY EGG

INGREDIENTS

14 ounces (400 g)
fresh udon noodles
1 and ½ cups (200 g) yam
2 spring onions
1 dried nori leaf
4 egg yolks
1 ½ tbsp. (20 g) wasabi paste

FOR DASHI
4 cups (1 l) water
10 g of kombu
3 tbsp. (20 g) katsuobushi (grated
dried bonito)
1 dried shiitake

Your mission accomplished and Nezuko, your sister, at your side, you take to the road again. No sooner do you slow down than a large black bird lands on your shoulder. The order of Demon Slayers summons you to investigate the Asakusa district in Tokyo. A few hours later, you arrive in the Japanese capital, your stomach hollow and your legs wobbly. A sweet smell of broth reaches your nostrils... Surely it would be better to begin your investigation with a stomach full of yam noodles?

✥ First prepare the dashi: pour the water into a saucepan, and add the kombu, the katsuobushi, and the shiitake. Bring to a simmer and cook for 30 minutes, but never bring to a boil.

✥ Meanwhile, prepare the remaining ingredients: peel the yam and grate it finely to obtain a thick, slightly syrupy purée. Set aside. Finely chop the spring onions. Cut the nori leaf into flakes.

✥ When you have finished making the broth, strain it to keep only the juice. (You can store the katsuobushi in the refrigerator for a few days and use it to season rice or fried eggs.) Pour the filtered broth into a saucepan and bring it to a simmer.

✥ In a big pot, bring a large volume of water to a boil and immerse the noodles for 12 minutes (traditionally, you should cook each portion of noodles separately). Drain them and rinse them in cold water for a few moments, separating them from each other with a chopstick. Set them aside for a few moments while you prepare the bowls.

In each bowl, first place a portion of noodles, then add hot dashi. On top of the noodles, place grated yam and egg yolk. Finish by adding the nori flakes, chopped spring onions, and a dab of wasabi. All that's left to do is to allow these noodles to warm your heart and soul. Just be careful not to drop your bowl...

LEVEL ✦
For 4 people
Preparation time: 15 min
Cooking time: 1 h 10

HANJI'S STEW
VEGETARIAN STEW

INGREDIENTS

FOR THE BROTH
14 and ½ cups (3,5 l) of water
1 leaf of kombu seaweed
2 dried shiitakes
3 tbsp. of soy sauce
1 bouquet garni (bundle of herbs tied with a string)
2 tbsp. tomato paste

FOR THE GARNISH
8 mashed potatoes
6 carrots
3 onions
8 large fresh button mushrooms or shiitakes
3 ½ ounces (100 g) peas or edamame beans
2 ounces (50 g) green beans

It is often impossible to get enemies to agree and fight together for a common goal. Tensions are high between the Eldians and the Marleyans, but you'll have to calm them down to fight Eren and prevent his genocidal plan. What if your makeshift stew could get everyone to share a moment of calm and restore their hope?

✣ First prepare the broth: pour the water, kombu seaweed, dried shiitakes, soy sauce, and bouquet garni into a pot. Bring to a low boil. Once boiling, remove the kombu seaweed and set aside over low heat.

✣ Next prepare the vegetables: wash the potatoes and carrots. Cut them into large irregular pieces. Peel the onions and cut them into large pieces. Clean the mushrooms with a slightly dampened paper towel and cut them in half. Rinse the peas or edamame. Rinse and remove the stems from the green beans.

✣ Drop all the vegetables into the broth and bring it back to the boil. Cover and continue to cook over medium heat for 1 hour.

✣ Ladle the broth into a large bowl. Add the tomato paste and dilute it in the broth, then pour the contents of the bowl into the casserole. Mix well and continue cooking for another 10 minutes: your stew is ready!

To serve, pour the broth and vegetables into 4 bowls and accompany with a slice of bread. These potatoes and bread soaked in broth will keep you going!

ONE PUNCH MAN

LEVEL ✦
For 2 people
Preparation time: 15 min
Cooking time: 25 min

NABE PUNCH
JAPANESE FONDUE WITH BEEF, TOFU, AND NAPA CABBAGE

INGREDIENTS

FOR THE BEEF
1 lb. and 5 ounces (600 g) beef steak
8 brown mushrooms or shiitakes
1 bunch of shimeji mushrooms
4 large Napa cabbage leaves
4 large handfuls of spinach shoots
7 ounces (200 g) firm tofu
3 ½ ounces (100 g) shirataki vermicelli
(or classic noodles)
Neutral vegetable oil

FOR THE SOY DASHI
6 cups and 4 tbsp. (1,5 l) water
⅓ ounce (10 g) kombu seaweed
1 tbsp. (5 g) katsuobushi
3 tbsp. of soy sauce
1 tbsp. mirin

FOR THE WARISHITA SAUCE
4 tbsp. of sake
4 tbsp. mirin
4 tbsp. soy sauce
1 tsp. pre-made soy dashi
1 tbsp. brown sugar

TO SERVE
Shichimi togarashi sancho pepper

The nabe! This is a dish that Saitama and Genos enjoy regularly. This fondue is a classic of Japanese cuisine, easy to prepare and to share. The trick is not to forget the cabbage leaves...

✤ Prepare the soy sauce dashi, the broth in which the ingredients will simmer: pour the water, the kombu seaweed, the katsuobushi, the soy sauce, and the mirin into a large saucepan and bring to a simmer. Simmer for 10 minutes before filtering the preparation to keep only the concentrated broth. Set aside.

✤ Next prepare the warishita sauce: pour the sake and mirin into a saucepan and bring to a gentle boil. Add the soy sauce, dashi, and sugar. Continue cooking for 2 minutes, stirring well, and set aside over very low heat. The warishita sauce is ready!

✤ Finally, prepare the nabemono: slice the beef very thinly. Using a slightly dampened paper towel, gently clean the mushrooms. Rinse and dry the vegetables. Drain the tofu and cut it into cubes.

✤ In a frying pan or in a nabe dish (also simply called a nabe, from the name of the dish), pour a good trickle of vegetable oil and heat over medium heat. Once the oil is hot, place the meat in it for a few moments, then evenly distribute the other ingredients around it. Moisten with the dashi and soy sauce and place your nabe or sauté pan on a baking sheet in the middle of the table. Continue cooking, covered, for 15 minutes.

Nabe is a sharing dish in which everyone helps themselves and cooks their ingredients in the broth. Season with warishita sauce, a few pinches of sansho pepper, and shichimi togarashi. Enjoy your meal!

NARUTO

LEVEL ✦ ✦ ✦
Preparation time: 45 min
Cooking time: 6 h 45 (including 6 h 30 for the chashu pork confit)
Rest time: 12 h (for the chashu pork confit)

THE BEST ICHIRAKU RAMEN

MISO CHASHU RAMEN

INGREDIENTS

11 ounces (320 g) wheat noodles
4 nice slices of narutomaki
1 ½ ounces (40 g) pickled bamboo shoots (menma)
2 spring onions, chopped
4 dried nori leaves
8 cups (2 l) broth (dashi, vegetable broth, chicken broth) (see Tips on pages 110-113)

FOR THE AROMATIC OIL
GARLIC AND GINGER

1 inch (3 cm) fresh ginger
1 clove of garlic
6 tbsp. and 2 tsp. (100 ml) neutral vegetable oil

FOR THE CHASHU PORK

1 lb. and 5 ounces (600 g) pork belly with skin, rolled and tied
4 shallots
2 cloves of garlic
⅔ inch (2 cm) fresh ginger
½ cup and 2 tbsp. (150 ml) soy sauce
1 cup (250 ml) cooking sake
1 cup (250 ml) mirin
6 tbsp. (75 g) brown sugar
1 ½ cup (350 ml) mineral water

Ichiraku ramen is definitely Naruto's favorite. With this recipe, you will discover the long process of turning them into bowls of happiness and umami!

✤ A ramen is made up of several elements: broth, noodles, tare (which gives the ramen its taste and signature), aromatic oil, and toppings. Each element you will make in this recipe can be frozen and stored for later. Here, you will learn how to make all the separate elements that go into the ramen. Once all these elements are ready, all you have to do is assemble them!

✤ First, prepare the aromatic oil: rinse, dry, and finely chop the ginger. Peel and finely chop the garlic. Pour the vegetable oil into a small saucepan and heat it to 176°F (80°C), then add the garlic and ginger. Brown them for 2 minutes, without burning them, before removing the pan from the heat. Let the aromatic oil cool and place it with the garlic and ginger pieces in an airtight container until needed.

✤ Next, prepare the pork chashu: peel and roughly chop the shallots. Crush the garlic and ginger, with their skin. Pour all the ingredients except the pork belly into a small cast-iron casserole dish (the pork belly should be perfectly immersed in the liquid, a casserole dish 18 cm in diameter should do the trick).

✤ Preheat the oven to 302°F (150°C / gas mark 2). Place the casserole over medium heat and bring to a gentle boil before plunging in the pork belly. Cover and bake for 1 hour and 30 minutes. Then lower the temperature to 266°F (130°C / gas mark 1) and continue cooking for 5 hours, turning over the meat in its juices halfway through the cooking time.

✤ Remove the casserole from the oven after cooking. Your meat should be tender and almost drying out before your eyes. You can eat it now, but for a more traditional result, let it rest for at least 12 hours in the refrigerator. This way, the meat will firm up and you will be able to cut it like ham.

Prepare the marinated eggs: bring a pot of water to a boil and immerse the eggs for 6 minutes. The eggs should be soft, the white is cooked but the yolk is still runny. While the eggs are cooking, prepare a container of ice water. Dip the cooked eggs in it to stop them from cooking. Peel them into the water directly to remove the shells more easily. Place the eggs in a small airtight container. Immerse them in the aromatic cooking juices of the chashu pork, add the water, and close the jar until ready to serve.

Next prepare the miso tare; be aware that there are different miso pastes, so feel free to test them out to find the one that suits you best. In a small bowl, mix all the ingredients with a whisk until you have a smooth mixture. Set aside.

Bring the broth to a simmer and whisk in the miso. Keep the broth at a simmer and prepare to serve your bowls of ramen.

Before you move on to cooking the noodles and putting all the ingredients together, make sure you have all the elements prepared and ready to assemble.

Take the eggs out of their marinade: they should be nicely colored and therefore seasoned.

Prepare the marinated bamboo slices. Thinly slice the chashu pork, allowing 2 slices per person. Take your aromatic oil. You are almost ready, the ramen is within your reach!

Bring 16 cups (4 l) of water to a boil and immerse the noodles in it. Cook them according to the packet instructions. When cooked, drain and rinse briefly under cold water to remove remaining starch and prevent sticking (traditionally, each portion of noodles should be cooked separately).

Now it's finally time to bring all the elements together! Pour a generous amount of hot miso broth in the bowl. Add 1 tsp. of aromatic oil and then add the noodles. Add a whole or sliced egg. Place the slices of chashu pork, then the bamboo slices, the sliced spring onions, and finally a sheet of nori along the side of the bowl. Finish by adding the slices of narutomaki. Your miso chashu ramen is ready, enjoy it immediately!

FOR THE PICKLED EGGS
4 eggs
2 ladles of the cooking juice from the chashu pork
2 tbsp. water

FOR MISO TARE
1 tbsp. miso paste
1 tbsp. mirin
1 tbsp. soy sauce
4 tbsp. water

ONE PIECE

LEVEL ✦
For 4 people
Preparation time: 20 min
Rest time: 1 to 12 h
Cooking time: 2 h 30
(45 min in a pressure cooker)

SANJI AND TAJIRO CURRY

JAPANESE CURRY

You may not look it, but you are one of the most seasoned and talented cooks on the Grand Line. So when you see a young cook in difficulty, you can't resist lending them a hand and teaching them how to cook a proper curry!

INGREDIENTS

1 tomato
4 carrots
4 potatoes
2 onions
8 cups (2 l) dried bonito dashi
(see Tips on page 110)
2 cups (0,5 l) of water
Vegetable oil
Salt, pepper

FOR THE BEEF AND MARINADE

1 lb. and 5 ounces (600 g) beef chuck
2 cloves of garlic
1/3 inch (1 cm) fresh ginger
1 tbsp. turmeric
4 tbsp. of yogurt
Salt, pepper

FOR THE CURRY POWDER

3 tbsp. (40 g) butter (or sunflower oil
for a vegan curry powder)
5 tbsp. (40 g) flour
1 tbsp. (10 g) curry powder
1 ½ tbsp. (15 g) garam masala
1 tsp. tomato paste
1 clove of garlic
1/3 inch (1 cm) of fresh ginger
2 tbsp. soy sauce
1 apple

TO SERVE

½ lb. and 3 ounces (320 g) pre-cooked
japonica or arborio rice

✠ First prepare the meat: cut it into medium-sized cubes and place it in a mixing bowl. Lightly season with salt and pepper. Set aside for a few moments. Peel and chop the garlic and ginger. Add them to the meat with the turmeric and the yogurt. Mix thoroughly: the lactic acid will make the meat tender. Cover with plastic wrap (clingfilm) and place in the refrigerator for a minimum of 1 hour and a maximum of 12 hours.

✠ While the meat is marinating, it's time to prepare the rest of the elements of your curry. Prepare a pot of boiling water and a large container of ice water. Slice the tomato with a paring knife, cut a cross at the base, and dip it into the boiling water for 30 seconds before plunging it into the ice water. Peel the tomato and cut it into quarters, then peel the carrots, potatoes, and onions. Cut the vegetables into large pieces and set them aside.

✠ Pour a good drizzle of vegetable oil into a casserole dish and heat over medium heat. Pour the marinated meat and the marinade into the pan and brown the pieces for 2 minutes. Add the tomato, carrots, potatoes, and onions, then add the dashi and water and mix well. Cover and let it simmer at a low boil for 2 hours.

✠ Now make the homemade curry powder. Melt the butter in a saucepan. Keep on low heat and add the flour, curry powder, garam masala, tomato paste, garlic, and ginger. Mix well until you get a smooth dried-out mixture and then add the soy sauce. Remove the pan from the heat. Coarsely grate the apple into the mixture. Return the pan to the heat and stir the apple into the curry powder. Once your mixture is smooth and sticks to the side of the pan, the powder is ready!

✠ Using a ladle, remove some of the cooking liquid from the meat and stir in the curry powder. Stir to combine the powder with the rest of the mixture. Continue cooking at a low boil for 30 to 45 minutes!

Serve generous portions of this curry into 4 soup bowls, accompanied with hot rice! Itadakimasu!

ONE PIECE

LEVEL ✦
For 4 people
Preparation time: 15 min
Cooking time: 15 min

GIN'S SEAFOOD RICE

RICE, OCTOPUS, AND FRIED PRAWNS

INGREDIENTS

2 spring onions
⅔ inch (2 cm) fresh ginger
1 lb. and 1 ½ once (500 g) calamari rings
2 squid tentacles cooked in court bouillon stock
8 organic prawns
2 tbsp. cooking sake
1 tbsp. soy sauce
10 ½ ounces (300 g) pre-cooked rice
1 tsp. shichimi togarashi
1 tbsp. nori powder
1 lemon
2 tbsp. vegetable oil

You discover the greatness of this cook, through a humble dish of rice sautéed with seafood, and you immediately want to make him the ship's chef!

✠ To begin, prepare the spring onions: finely slice the green part and chop the bulb. Put them aside separately. Peel and chop the ginger.

✠ Next prepare the seafood: rinse the squid rings. Cut the tentacles into small pieces. Shell and devein the prawns.

✠ In a large frying pan or wok, pour in the vegetable oil and heat over high heat. Once the oil is hot, add the squid rings and stir-fry for 4 to 5 minutes. Deglaze with sake and soy sauce. Add the white of the onions and ginger and reduce the heat to medium. Add the squid tentacles and prawns. Fry them for 1 min 30 with the rings. Add the rice and season with shichimi togarashi and nori powder. Return to high heat and sauté for 1.5 to 2 minutes before serving hot.

✠ Garnish with green onion for a little freshness and sprinkle with a little lemon juice before serving. This seafood rice dish will bring you to life!

JOJO'S BIZARRE
ADVENTURE

LEVEL ✦
For 4 people
Preparation time: 10 min
Cooking time: 15 min

TONIO'S PRIMO PIATTO

PASTA WITH PUTTANESCA

INGREDIENTS

10 anchovy fillets with salt
1 clove of garlic
13 cups (3,2 l) water
2 tbsp. (32 g) coarse salt
½ lb. (250 g) peeled San Marzano
or datterini tomatoes
20 organic black olives
from Nice or Gaeta
2 tbsp. capers
2 pinches of red pepper
(from Calabria if possible)
½ lb. and 3 ounces (320 g) spaghetti
½ bunch of fresh flat-leaf parsley
6 tbsp. (60 g) parmesan cheese
Olive oil
Salt, pepper

This typical pasta dish is so hot and delicious that it will make your jaw drop and your teeth pop!

✤ Rinse and dry the anchovy fillets. Peel and finely chop the garlic. Pour the water into a large pot and add the coarse salt. Bring to a boil.

✤ While the water is boiling, pour 2 tbsp. of olive oil into a large skillet and place over medium heat. Add the garlic and sauté for 1 minute until brown. Add the anchovies and sauté for 2 minutes before adding the tomatoes. Mix well and add the black olives, capers, and pinches of red pepper. Mix well and let it simmer over low heat.

✤ Once the water is boiling, add the spaghetti without breaking it and cook it for a few minutes, according to the packet instructions, until it is al dente. Once the pasta is cooked, add it directly from to the sauce.

Serve the pasta hot with a few leaves of flat-leaf parsley. Grate the parmesan cheese and sprinkle it over the pasta before eating!

LEVEL ✦
For 4 people
Preparation time: 20 min
Rest time: 1 h
Cooking time: 20 min

BLACK INK TAGLIATELLE

TAGLIATELLE WITH CUTTLEFISH INK

INGREDIENTS

FOR HOMEMADE TAGLIATELLE
3 cups (400 g) flour
4 whole eggs
1 pinch of salt
1 tsp. cuttlefish ink paste

FOR THE CUTTLEFISH
4 cloves of garlic
2 shallots
½ bunch of parsley
1 tsp. cuttlefish ink paste
1 small cuttlefish gutted and
prepared by your fishmonger
Olive oil
2 tbsp. (30 g) butter
Salt, pepper

You will always remember your first encounter with Caesar Antonio Zeppelli; the dastardly flirt was having the time of his life, charming a young woman who was lapping up his words. You couldn't resist using your pasta to secretly go after him… That pasta was pretty good, why not try to reproduce it?

✠ Start by making the pasta: pour the flour on your work surface and make a large well in the center. Break the eggs into a bowl and pour them into the center of the well. Use a fork to mix the flour into the eggs for 2-4 minutes until the mixture is smooth. Sprinkle with 1 pinch of salt. Add the cuttlefish ink paste and knead with the palms of your hands for 10 minutes, until the dough is dark and smooth. Place in a bowl, cover with plastic wrap (clingfilm) and refrigerate for 1 hour.

✠ Divide the dough into quarters. Roll out the dough pieces into 4 thin, long strips. Fold each strip back on itself several times and, using a chef's knife, cut them widthwise to make the tagliatelle. Spread them out on a sheet of parchment paper, covered with a little flour to prevent them from sticking. Set them aside for a few moments.

✠ Now prepare the cuttlefish. Peel the garlic and shallots. Chop them finely. Do the same with the parsley: remove the leaves and chop them. Put the cuttlefish ink paste in 2 cups (500 ml) of water and stir until it is diluted. Cut the cuttlefish into strips.

✠ Pour 1 drizzle of olive oil into a frying pan and heat over medium heat. Add 2 tbsp. (30 g) butter and, when it has melted, sauté the chopped shallot for 2 minutes. Add the garlic and half the parsley. Fry for 1 more minute before turning up the heat and adding the cuttlefish strips. Sprinkle with 1 pinch of salt and sauté for 1 min before deglazing with the cuttlefish ink water. Mix well and bring to a simmer. Reduce the sauce by half (about 10 minutes).

✠ Meanwhile, bring 12 cups (3 l) of salted water to a boil and plunge the tagliatelle into it for 2 to 3 min. Using tongs, while the pasta is still a bit firm, remove it and place it immediately in the pan containing the cuttlefish and sauce. Coat the tagliatelle well with the sauce and add the remaining parsley.

To serve, spoon strips of cuttlefish into the center of 4 soup plates. Arrange the cuttlefish ink tagliatelle on top. All that's left to do is enjoy your meal!

EQUIPMENT

Rolling mill

BORUTO

LEVEL ✦
For 4 people
Preparation time: 30 min
Cooking time: 10 min

SUPER-BITTER BURGER

CHICKEN BURGER WITH LEMON MAYONNAISE AND CANDIED LEMON

INGREDIENTS

4 homemade burger buns
(see Tips on page 115)
4 lettuce leaves
2 whole candied lemons
1 ¾ tbsp. (25 g) butter
Olive oil
Salt

FOR THE CHICKEN STEAKS
10 ½ ounces (300 g) ground poultry
1/3 inch (1 cm) of ginger
1 egg
2 tbsp. breadcrumbs
2 tbsp. milk
1 level tsp. of salt
1 level tsp. of paprika

FOR THE SAUCE
10 fresh coriander or dill leaves
4 tbsp. mayonnaise
The juice of ½ lemon
1 level tsp. of ground
sansho pepper

If Naruto is crazy about ramen, his son is much more passionate about mysterious art and... eating burgers! Here is one of the famous recipes from Kaminari Burger, a sandwich that he had the pleasure to taste with Konohoamaru and Miss Remon: the super-bitter burger!

✤ First, prepare the chicken steaks: peel and finely chop the ginger. Place it in a bowl with the ground chicken, egg, breadcrumbs, milk, salt, and paprika. Mix thoroughly until smooth.

✤ Lightly flour your hands and separate the filling into 4 equal pieces. Shape them into steaks in the palm of your hand, then move them from one hand to the other to get the air out, so that they will be solid when cooked. Plastic wrap (clingfilm) and keep in the refrigerator while you prepare the rest of the ingredients.

✤ Chop the cilantro or dill in a bowl. Add the mayonnaise, lemon juice, and sansho pepper. Mix well.

✤ Rinse, dry, and coarsely chop the lettuce. Mince the candied lemons. Your elements are ready, so go ahead and cook!

✤ Brush the insides of the loaves with butter and place in a pan over medium heat to brown them. Remove from the heat when golden brown.

✤ Drizzle vegetable oil into a large skillet and heat over high heat. Place the chicken steaks in the pan and sprinkle with a good pinch of salt. Let them grill for 1 minute per side before lowering the heat and cooking them for 6 to 8 minutes so that they are well-melted but cooked through. Remove them to a paper towel.

For each burger, brush the buttered buns with sauce. Place a chicken steak on top, and cover with slices of candied lemon and chopped salad. Enjoy.

BORUTO

LEVEL ✦

For 4 people
Preparation time: 30 min
Rest time: 1 h
Cooking time: 10 min

THE ULTRA-SPICY BURGER

HAMBAGU-STYLE STEAK BURGER WITH CHILI KETCHUP

INGREDIENTS

4 homemade burger buns
(see Tips on page 115)
Paprika or ground cayenne pepper
4 salad leaves or shiso
16 small peppers
4 slices of pickle or cucumber
Sesame oil
Vegetable oil (olive, grape seed)

FOR THE HAMBAGU STUFFING
1 large onion
½ lb. (250 g) ground beef
5 ounces (150 g) ground pork
1 egg
A small tsp. (5 g) of salt
2 tbsp. of veal stock on ice
(see Tips on page 111)
1 tsp. red miso
2 tbsp. panko breadcrumbs
2 tbsp. milk
1 tsp. nori powder or flat parsley

FOR THE CHILI KETCHUP
4 tbsp. homemade ketchup
(see Tip page 114)
2 tbsp. of chili paste (or more
if you like it spicy!)
1 tsp. soy sauce
1 tsp. brown sugar

Here is the burger that made Boruto's mouth water: the Hot'n Spicy burger. It's so strong that it makes you cry just sniffing it… We still wonder if any human can really take it…

✠ First prepare the stuffing. Peel and finely chop the onion. Pour a small amount of vegetable oil into a frying pan and heat it over medium heat. Fry the chopped onion for 5 minutes without caramelizing it too much. Set aside. Combine the ground beef and pork, egg, salt, veal juice with ice, miso, panko breadcrumbs, milk, nori powder, and onion in a bowl. Using your hands, mix the ingredients thoroughly for 2 minutes until you obtain a thick and smooth filling.

✠ Next shape the steaks: separate the stuffing into 4 equal pieces. Lightly oil your hands with a drop of sesame oil and shape the steaks by passing them from one hand to the other, as if you were juggling a ball: this expels the air contained in the steaks to ensure that they do not burst during cooking. Place in a dish and cover with plastic wrap (clingfilm).

✠ Set aside for 1 hour in the refrigerator to allow the fats to set before cooking.

✠ Meanwhile, prepare the chili ketchup: in a bowl, mix the ketchup, chili paste, soy sauce, and sugar.

✠ Broil or toast the loaves. Using the stencil (see page 115), sprinkle paprika or ground chili pepper onto the top loaf.

✠ Drizzle a good amount of vegetable oil into a skillet and heat over high heat. Place the steaks in the hot pan and grill for a good minute on each side before lowering the heat to medium. Continue cooking for 4-5 minutes and then remove the steaks to paper towels.

✠ Coat the toasted buns with chili ketchup and then assemble your burgers in this order, from bottom to top: the coated bun, a leaf of lettuce or shiso, the steak, the sauce, the pickles, the whole chilies, and finally the bun. Enjoy immediately!

Note: this recipe is moderately spicy. Be aware that excessive consumption of fresh and strong chili can be dangerous. So be careful, you have been warned!

HUNTER X HUNTER
LEVEL ✦
For 4 people
Preparation time: 15 min
Cooking time: 1 h 50

PASTA FROM DOPFF AU MOULIN
SPAGHETTI, RAGÙ, AND MUSHROOMS

INGREDIENTS

11 ½ ounces (320 g) of spaghetti
1 stalk of celery
2 carrots
4 shallots
10 button mushrooms
½ lb. (250 g) ground beef
5 ounces (150 g) ground pork
or ground veal
1 tbsp. ground thyme
1 tbsp. dried oregano
7 tbsp. (10 cl) white wine
7 tbsp. (10 cl) veal juice
2 cups (500 g) organic tomato pulp
1 cup (150 g) canned
datterini tomatoes
1 pinch of sugar
1 bouquet garni (bundle of herbs tied
with a string)
4 tbsp. (60 ml) whole milk
1 tbsp. and 2 tsp. (30 g)
coarse grey salt
A few basil leaves
Olive oil
Salt, pepper

Few people are up to your pasta challenge: to devour a mountain of spaghetti in sauce in less than 30 minutes! These two boys, Gon and Kirua, surprised you by doing it in only a few minutes... How can such small people manage to eat so much food?

✤ First prepare the sofrito: the Italian-style aromatic garnish. Cut the celery, carrots, and shallots into a fine brunoise (cubes of about 3 mm on each side). Set aside. Peel and slice the mushrooms.

✤ Finely salt each ground meat separately and add to a mixing bowl with the thyme and oregano.

✤ In a large frying pan, pour a good drizzle of olive oil and heat over medium heat. Add the diced vegetables and season lightly. Brown them for 20 minutes before removing to a bowl.

✤ Place the pan over high heat and brown the meat on all sides for 1 to 2 minutes. Deglaze with white wine. Scrape the bottom of the pan with a wooden spatula to loosen the juices.

✤ Stir the vegetables back into the meat, then add the veal juice and tomatoes. Add sugar, mix well, and adjust the seasoning to your taste. Add the bouquet garni, lower the heat, and simmer the sauce al ragù for 1 hour and a half. At the end of the cooking time, add the milk to the sauce and mix well.

✤ When the sauce is almost ready, prepare the pasta: pour 13 cups (3,2 l) of water into a large pot, add the coarse salt, and bring to a boil. Add the pasta and cook for 30 seconds to 1 minute less than the time indicated on the package. Remove 2 ladles of the cooking water. Drain the spaghetti and plunge it in the simmering al ragù sauce, then add in the 2 ladles of cooking water. Mix carefully so that the pasta soaks in the sauce and finishes cooking in it. Serve hot and sprinkle a few basil leaves on top!

FIRE FORCE

LEVEL ✦ ✦
For 1 person
Preparation time: 10 min
Cooking time: 12 min

ISARIBI OMURICE
SPICY STIR-FRIED RICE, OMELETTE
AND HOMEMADE KETCHUP

INGREDIENTS

FOR THE OMELETTE
3 eggs
1 good pinch of salt
1 tbsp. (15 g) of butter

FOR THE SAUTÉED RICE
1 ½ ounces (50 g) steamed rice
3 tbsp. (20 g) cooked peas
1 spring onion
2 large mushrooms
5 cherry tomatoes
2 tbsp. soy sauce
1 tbsp. mirin
1 tsp. chili purée
A pinch of sugar
Olive oil
Salt, pepper

TO SERVE
Homemade ketchup
(see Tips on page 114)
Cherry tomatoes
Fresh cucumber

Lisa has a knack for cooking a delicious omurice from leftovers. It is a dish that reminds us of family memories and makes us want to spend time with the people we love...

✤ First, make the rice stir-fry: chop the spring onion and separate the green parts from the white. Clean the mushrooms with a slightly damp paper towel and cut them into 2 mm cubes. Cut the tomatoes in half.

✤ Pour a drizzle of olive oil into a pan and heat over medium heat. Place the tomatoes in the pan. Sprinkle with a pinch of salt and sugar and fry for 5 minutes. Add the rice and dehusk it. Fry it and add the onion and mushrooms. Add the soy sauce, mirin, and chili paste and mix well. Increase the heat slightly and stir-fry for 2 minutes before setting the stir-fried rice and vegetables aside in a large bowl.

✤ Prepare the omelette: beat the eggs in a bowl without foaming the mixture. Add salt to taste. Set aside for a few moments. Put the butter in a frying pan and place over medium heat. Once the butter has melted, pour in the omelette mixture and cook for 1 min 30 to 2 min. Use a wooden spatula to loosen the omelet from the sides of the pan. Roll the omelet in on itself so that it takes a rectangular shape. It should look like a small quilt that covers the rice.

✤ To serve, fill bowls with rice and turn them upside down on your plate to create rice domes. Use peas and some nori leaf flakes to create an image of the eyes, nose, and whiskers of a seal pup. Cover the rice with the omelet and top with homemade ketchup. Serve with some fresh vegetables and enjoy hot!

TOKYO GHOUL

LEVEL ✦
For 4 people
Preparation time: 15 min
Cooking time: 1 hour

YORIKO'S NIKUJAGA

BEEF AND VEGETABLE STEW WITH SHIRATAKI

INGREDIENTS

2 carrots
2 onions
8 potatoes, mashed
3 ½ ounces (100 g) peas
10 ½ ounces (300 g) konjac shirataki
1 lb. and 5 ounces (600 g) pork tenderloin, beef miter, or chicken fillet
6 tbsp. and 2 tsp. (100 ml) soy sauce
3 tbsp. and 1 tsp. (50 ml) mirin
3 tbsp. and 1 tsp. (50 ml) cooking sake
2 tsp. powdered sugar
Salt, pepper
2 cups (500 ml) dashi (see Tips on page 110)
Sesame oil

Nikujaga is a Japanese comfort food, the perfect dish for someone you love who is not feeling well – a dish that Yoriko masters perfectly!

✤ First, prepare the vegetables: peel the carrots and cut them into large, even pieces. Peel the onions and cut them into quarters. Peel the potatoes and cut them in half. Rinse the peas well.

✤ Bring a pot of lightly salted water to a boil and immerse the shirataki in it for 3 minutes. Drain them.

✤ Slice the meat into thin strips. Everything is ready, move on to cooking.

✤ Drizzle a good amount of sesame oil into a casserole dish and place over medium heat. Add the meat and season it finely. Fry for 2 minutes before adding the onions, carrots, and potatoes. Sauté for 2 minutes and then add the soy sauce, mirin, sake, and sugar. Mix well. Gather the shirataki into a block and cut them into quarters before adding them to the pot. Pour in the dashi broth.

✤ Reduce heat to low and simmer covered for 30 minutes. Add the peas and cook for another 10 minutes. Everything is ready: serve directly in the casserole if you prefer!

MY HERO ACADEMIA

LEVEL ✦
For 1 katsudon
Preparation time: 15 min
Rest time: 30 min
Cooking time: 30 min

MOM'S KATSUDON

BREADED PORK CHOP, BEATEN EGG IN SAUCE AND SUSHI RICE

INGREDIENTS

3 ½ ounces (100 g) sushi rice

FOR THE TONKATSU PORK
1 boneless pork chop
(or 1 small cutlet)
1 egg + 1 egg yolk
Fine breadcrumbs or panko
Oil for frying
Salt and pepper

FOR THE SAUCE
AND SCRAMBLED EGG
1 spring onion
Sunflower oil
1 tbsp. soy sauce
1 tsp. rice or cider vinegar
1 tsp. ketchup
1 egg

Despite intensive training, it's still very difficult to use the power of One for All without getting hurt and suffering the consequences. With the super villains joining forces, you'll have to learn to master this power and keep your spirits up. Nothing better for that than a hot katsudon, just how mom makes it!

✠ Start by preparing the sushi rice. It is important to rinse it well several times. Put it in a container and run it under cold water. Knead the rice, rub it between your hands, remove the water, then put it back and repeat until the water is clear. At this point, cover the rice with water and let it sit for 30 minutes at room temperature.

✠ After the resting time, drain the rice and place it in a saucepan. Add 6 tbsp. and 2 tsp. (100 ml) of water, cover the pan, and bring to a boil over medium heat. Cook the rice for 10 minutes, covered, then remove the pan from the heat and let the rice continue cooking for another 10 minutes.

✠ Move onto preparing the breaded pork: cut the edges of the cutlet 1 cm every 2 cm. Use a rolling pin to tap the meat to flatten it and make it tender. Sprinkle the meat with a good pinch of salt.

✠ Place the whole egg, the yolk and the white, in a shallow dish and beat with a fork. Pour breadcrumbs into a second soup plate. Dip the meat in the beaten egg first, then place it in the breadcrumbs so that it is perfectly covered.

✠ In a saucepan, heat the frying oil over high heat until it reaches 356°F (180°C / gas mark 4). Dip the pork into the boiling oil for 2 minutes, taking care not to burn yourself, then turn it over and cook for another 2 minutes. With tongs, remove the breaded pork from the oil and place it on a paper towel, then cut it into slices following the notches made before having breaded it. Set aside.

✠ Prepare the sauce and scrambled egg: rinse the spring onion and remove its stalks. Cut the green parts into thin strips and the white into thin slices. Pour a dash of sunflower oil into a small pan and heat over medium heat. Once the pan is hot, add the soy sauce, vinegar and ketchup and mix well. Add the onion slices and cook for 2 minutes, then place the breaded pork on top. Lightly beat the egg in a bowl and pour it over the sauce and breaded pork, then cover the pan. Continue cooking for another minute or so and remove the pan from the heat.

To serve, place the hot rice on a soup plate and the breaded pork on top, with the cooked beaten egg and sauce. Sprinkle with the green parts of the onion to add a dash of color.

SEVEN DEADLY SINS

LEVEL ✦ ✦
For 4 people
Preparation time: 30 min
Cooking time: 35 min

BOAR HAT PIE

MEAT AND VEGETABLE PIE

INGREDIENTS

2 carrots
1 mashed potato
3 tbsp. peas
1 onion
½ lb. (250 g) ground beef
½ lb. (250 g) ground pork
1 whole egg + 1 yolk
1 tsp. garlic powder
1 tsp. thyme
1 tsp. salt
½ tsp. pepper
2 tbsp. flour
1 tbsp. olive oil
1 tbsp. and 1 tsp. butter
3 ounces (80 g) smoked bacon
1 cup (250 ml) beef broth
(see Tip page 111)
1 tsp. cornstarch
2 rolls of organic shortcrust pastry

The Boar Hat, Meliodas' traveling inn, is famous for the quality of the drinks it serves, but not at all for the quality of the food that comes out of the kitchen. Its meat pie is not necessarily to the taste of its customers. Here's the recipe they need!

✠ Start by preparing the vegetables: peel and dice the carrots and potatoes. Rinse the peas. Bring a pot of salted water to a boil and immerse the vegetables for 15 minutes. Drain and set aside.

✠ While the vegetables are cooking, prepare the meat filling: peel the onion and cut it into thin strips. Place the minced meat in a bowl. Add the whole egg, garlic powder, thyme, salt and pepper and mix until you have a smooth ball. Sprinkle the meat with flour until it is perfectly coated.

✠ Heat a saucepan over medium heat, then pour in the olive oil and add the butter. Once the butter has melted and the oil is hot, add the onions and sauté for 5 minutes, until they turn a nice golden color. Add the smoked bacon and continue cooking for 5 minutes.

✠ Place the floured meat ball in the hot pan and press it lightly so that it covers the entire bottom of the pan. Let it cook for 2 minutes before turning it over. Cook for another 2 minutes before using a wooden spoon to break up the meat into small pieces. Pour the beef broth into the pan and sprinkle with 1 tbsp. of flour. Mix well and continue cooking for another 5 minutes.

✠ Preheat the oven to 356°F (180°C / gas mark 4).

✠ Using a skimmer, remove the meat from the pan and place it in a bowl. Add the diced potato, carrot, and peas. Save the cooking juices for the sauce.

✠ Heat the meat juices over medium heat for 10 minutes, then add 1 tbsp. of butter. Let it melt while stirring carefully. Finally, sprinkle 1 tsp. of cornstarch into the liquid and mix well. Lower the heat and simmer for the time it takes to prepare the pie.

✠ Generously butter a pie pan. Line it with a roll of shortcrust pastry, pressing it firmly against the sides. Pour the meat and vegetable mixture onto the dough. Moisten with 4 tbsp. of the meat juice and cover with a second roll of shortcrust pastry. Press the edges of the dough together to close the pie and, with a knife or cookie cutter, make a 2 cm diameter hole in the center. This hole will allow the steam to escape during the cooking process. Feel free to draw patterns in the dough with a fork or the tip of a knife.

✠ Finally, mix the egg yolk with 2 tbsp. of water and, with a glaze brush, brush it on the pie. Bake for 35 to 40 minutes. Take the pie out of the oven. It is better to let it cool a little before eating it!

FOODWARS!

LEVEL ✦
For 4 people
Preparation time: 40 min
Rest time: 15 min
Cooking time: 35 min

REVISITED ROAST

POTATO ROAST

INGREDIENTS

FOR THE ROAST
8 mashed potatoes
6 large shiitakes
or button mushrooms
1 onion
Olive oil
Soft butter
Salt, pepper, nutmeg
6 tbsp. and 2 tsp. (100 ml) milk
A few sprigs of fresh rosemary
16 slices of smoked bacon

FOR THE RED WINE SAUCE
1 shallot
1 ½ tbsp. (20 g) soft butter
2 cups (450 ml) red wine
3 tbsp. and 1 tsp. (50 ml) of sweet sake
½ cup and 5 tbsp. (200 ml)
of veal stock
½ tsp. cornstarch

No more backing down! Here's a recipe that will make you a legend, even if your pantry has been cleaned out.

✤ Begin by preparing the vegetables: peel the potatoes, cut them into irregular cubes, and plunge them into a bowl filled with water.

✤ Using a lightly dampened paper towel, gently clean the mushrooms, then chop them finely. Peel and finely chop the onion. Set the onion and mushrooms aside.

✤ Place the potato cubes in a pot of salted water or in a pressure cooker: cook for 20 minutes after boiling or 15 minutes as soon as the pressure cooker valve begins to whistle.

✤ Meanwhile, pour a drizzle of olive oil into a frying pan and heat over medium heat: add the chopped onion and a knob of butter. Sauté the onion over medium heat for 5 minutes before adding the mushrooms. Fry for 5 minutes and remove the water from the mushrooms. Add a little salt and continue cooking over low heat for another 10 minutes, then set aside.

✤ Once the potatoes are cooked, drain them and place them in a mixing bowl. Season them to taste with salt, pepper, and nutmeg; add the milk and 20 g of butter. Using a fork or potato masher, mash the potatoes until you have a creamy mixture that is not entirely smooth – it should still contain a few solid pieces. Stir in the onion/mushroom mix. The mixture is ready: film it and place it in the refrigerator for 15 minutes. Preheat the oven to 356°F (180 °C / gas mark 4).

✤ After 15 minutes, take your mashed potatoes. Shape it like a roast and place a few sprigs of rosemary on the surface. Evenly coat the roast with slices of smoked bacon. Tie the whole thing up with cooking string, place the roast in an ovenproof dish and bake for 35 minutes.

✤ Meanwhile, make the red wine sauce: peel and chop the shallot. Place a saucepan over medium heat, add a knob of butter and, once melted, add the chopped shallot. Sweat for 2 minutes before deglazing with red wine and sake. Bring to a boil and flambé the mixture. Add the veal stock and cornstarch and reduce to glaze, i.e. for about 15 minutes until the mixture takes on a syrupy texture.

Place the «roast» on a serving dish, remove the string, and pour the red wine and sake sauce over it. Itadakimasu!

JET'S BEEF
CHINJAO ROSU: BEEF SAUTÉED WITH VEGETABLES

LEVEL ✦
For 4 people
Preparation time: 20 min
Rest time: 1 h
Cooking time: 10 to 15 minutes

INGREDIENTS

1 ½ cups and 3 tbsp. (400 ml) soy sauce
½ cup and 5 tbsp. (200 ml) sake
½ cup and 5 tbsp. (200 ml)
black sesame oil
1 tsp. pepper
1 lb. and 5 ounces (600 g) beef
or whiting steak
4 green peppers
2 onions
1 clove of garlic
⅓ ounce (10 g) ginger

EQUIPMENT

Wok

While Spike is training on his own, why not take the opportunity to cook one of your favorite recipes, Chinjao Rosu? And luckily, this time you actually have some beef!

✤ Start by preparing the meat and its marinade: pour ½ cup and 5 tbsp. (200 ml) soy sauce, 7 tbsp. (100 ml) sake and 3 tbsp. and 1 tsp. (50 ml) black sesame oil into a bowl. Crush the pepper, add it to the liquid ingredients and mix together.

✤ Slice the steak into thin strips and place them in the marinade you have just prepared. Mix well so that the marinade is perfectly absorbed by the meat. Place in the refrigerator for 1 hour.

✤ Now prepare the vegetables: remove the seeds and chop the peppers. Peel and chop the onions. Peel and chop the garlic and ginger.

✤ Pour 3 tbsp. and 1 tsp. (50 ml) of black sesame oil in your wok and heat over medium heat. Once the wok is hot, place the vegetables, garlic, and ginger in the wok and stir-fry them for 5 minutes, until they are crisp. Remove and drizzle black sesame oil into the wok.

✤ Heat for a few moments before adding the marinated meat slices: sauté for 2 to 5 minutes according to your taste, before adding the sautéed vegetables. Season with the remaining soy sauce, sake, and sesame oil.

✤ Sauté for an additional 2 minutes while stirring well with chopsticks or a wooden spatula. Serve and enjoy hot.

DESSERTS

&

DRINKS

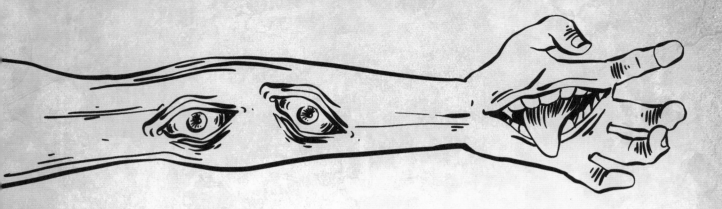

LEVEL ✦ ✦ ✦
For 10 mochis
Preparation time: 45 min
Cooking time: 15 min
Rest time: 40 min

GOJO'S KIKUFUKU
SWEETENED CREAM AND EDAMAME MOCHI

INGREDIENTS

FOR THE EDAMAME CREAM
7 ounces (200 g) edamame beans
8 cups (2 l) sparkling water
2 ½ tbsp. (30 g) sugar
⅔ tsp. (4 g) salt

FOR THE WHIPPED CREAM
1 cup (250 ml) whipping cream
30 % M.F. minimum
2 ½ cups (20 g) powdered sugar

FOR THE MOCHI DOUGH
½ cup (120 g) shiratamako
(glutinous rice flour)
½ a cup (100 g) white sugar
1 cup (250 ml) water
Corn starch

You will always remember your encounter with Satoru Gojo: you had just eaten a special grade relic, releasing a terribly dangerous plague to the world. Mr. Gojo had been sent to control this threat and it was with a bag of Sendai kikufuku that he arrived on the scene to deal with the problem. He had been to buy mochis from Kikusuian to have something to eat after taking care of you...

✤ First, prepare the cream. Peel the beans. Bring the sparkling water to a boil and immerse the beans in it. Cook them for 10 minutes. While they are cooking, prepare a large volume of ice water. Plunge the beans into the ice water to stop the cooking process and then peel off the last of the skin.

✤ Blend the cooked beans with a blender (herb or hand blender). Add 1 to 2 tbsp. of water to help combine the ingredients and to give the mixture a smooth texture. Place in a saucepan, then add the sugar and salt. Mix well and cook over medium heat for 5 minutes, stirring constantly, until the water has evaporated. Pour the cream into a large container. Let it cool for 15 minutes before sealing it and placing it in the refrigerator for 15 minutes.

✤ In the meantime, prepare the whipped cream: pour the whipping cream into a bowl and whip vigorously until it begins to stiffen. Add the powdered sugar and continue to whip until you have a thick, firm cream. Place in a piping bag and keep in the refrigerator.

✤ Line silicone ice cube molds with edamame cream and create a small hole in the middle. Fill each hole with whipped cream and cover with the remaining edamame cream. Cover with foil and place in the freezer for 10 minutes, then in the refrigerator for another 10 minutes.

✤ Meanwhile, prepare the dough: combine the flour and sugar in a microwave-safe container. While mixing, pour in the water. Plastic wrap (clingfilm) the dish and place in the microwave for 1 min 30 at 850 W. Lift the film, mix quickly and replace the film. Repeat the cooking and mixing process twice more until you have a smooth and very sticky mixture.

✤ Next cover a baking sheet with cornstarch and place the mochi dough on top. Sprinkle the dough lightly with cornstarch to prevent sticking and roll out with a rolling pin to a thickness of 2 to 3 mm. Cut out discs of the dough with a circular cookie cutter. Lightly moisten each disc of dough.

✤ Turn the edamame cream «candies» out of the molds and place them in the center of each dough disk. Close the dough and shape them quickly in the palm of your hand to give them a nice round shape. Your kikufuku are ready!

LEVEL ✦ ✦

For 4 taiyaki

Preparation time: 10 min

Rest time: 1 h

Cooking time: 5 min

GRAN TORINO'S TAIYAKI

STUFFED WAFFLES, ANKO BATTER

INGREDIENTS

2 tbsp. (25 g) sugar

1 small tbsp. (10 g) vanilla sugar

2 eggs

1 cup (150 g) flour T65

½ packet of baking powder

1 pinch of salt

10 tbsp. (150 ml) milk

1 tbsp. and 1 tsp. (20 ml)
of neutral vegetable oil

4 ounces (120 g) homemade
anko dough (see Tips on page 116)
or any store-bought anko dough

EQUIPMENT

Taiyaki mold

Taiyaki is Gran Torino's favorite pastry! Here's how to make taiyaki in the traditional way so that you can enjoy it hot, just like the old man!

✜ First, prepare your taiyaki dough. Pour the sugars into a bowl and add the eggs. Whisking vigorously, whiten the eggs, then add the flour, yeast, and salt. While whisking, add the milk and oil until you have a smooth mixture. Leave to rest for 1 hour.

✜ Now it's time to start cooking. Heat the taiyaki pan over high heat and then turn down to medium heat. Pour a small ladleful of taiyaki batter into the pan and place 1 teaspoon full of anko batter in the middle of the batter. Cover with taiyaki mixture and close the pan.

✜ Cook for 1 to 1 ½ minutes before turning the pan over (holding it firmly and being careful not to burn yourself). Continue cooking for 1 to 1.5 minutes, then remove the taiyaki from the pan and place it on a rack.

✜ Repeat until all ingredients are used up.

Enjoy these hot taiyaki and get back to training, you won't master One for All by standing still!

FAIRY TAIL

LEVEL ✦
For 4 people
Preparation time: 20 min
Cooking time: 30 min

FANTASIA CAKE

GENOISE WITH VANILLA WHIPPED CREAM AND FRESH STRAWBERRIES

INGREDIENTS

FOR THE SPONGE CAKE
4 eggs
½ cup (125 g) sugar
2 tbsp. (30 g) of soft butter
1 cup (125 g) of flour

FOR THE WHIPPED CREAM
4 cups (1 l) cold whipping cream
(over 30 % fat)
1 tsp. coffee vanilla extract
1 small cup (100 g) powdered sugar

TO SERVE
2 cups (300 g) fresh strawberries
Zest of 1 lime

Many have lost to Erza in single combat, others by simply standing between her and a piece of Fantasia cake...Here's how to make her favorite dessert.

✤ Preheat the oven to 356°F (180°C / gas mark 4) and place the bowl and the beaters of your electric mixer in the refrigerator.

✤ Start by preparing the sponge cake: place the eggs and sugar in a mixing bowl or in the bowl of a food processor. Whip vigorously with an electric whisk or the whisk attachment of the food processor for 10 minutes. The mixture should be well whitened and have doubled in volume.

✤ Melt the butter in a microwave or in a saucepan over low heat and set aside. Using a spatula, add the flour to the fluffy mixture, though gently so as not to break up the airy effect. Then add the butter in the same way.

✤ Butter a round cake tin and pour the mixture inside. Bake for 25 to 30 minutes. Your sponge cake is now ready. Let it cool down.

✤ Next take the mixing bowl that you placed in the refrigerator. Pour in the whipping cream and vanilla extract. Using a hand whisk, electric whisk or food processor, whip the cream vigorously. Whip for 3 minutes and add the powdered sugar while whisking. Your cream is ready when it is firm. Put it in a piping bag and set aside for a few moments.

✤ Clean the strawberries under a thin stream of water. Dry them with a paper towel. Hull the strawberries.

✤ Now you have all your ingredients, it is time to put them together. Turn out the sponge cake and cut it in half. Top one part with a first layer of vanilla whipped cream and fresh strawberries. Cover with the other part of the sponge cake and repeat with a second layer of cream and strawberries. Finally, add the lime zest on top of the strawberries, and voilà!

FANTASIA
4500J

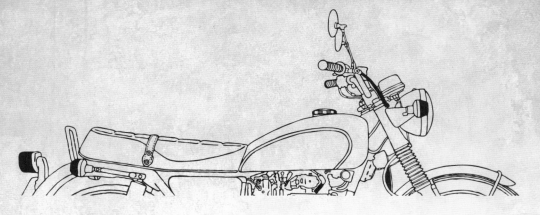

TOKYO REVENGERS

LEVEL ✦
For 4 people
Preparation time: 20 min
Cooking time: 10 min

MIKEY'S DORAYAKI

DORAYAKI, PEANUT BUTTER, AND BLACK SESAME WHIPPED CREAM

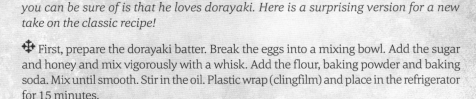

INGREDIENTS

FOR THE DORAYAKI DOUGH
3 eggs
9 tbsp. (120 g) sugar
1 tbsp. honey
1 cup and 2 tbsp. (140 g) flour
2 ½ tsp. (11 g) baking powder
1 pinch of baking soda
1 tsp. coffee of neutral vegetable oil

FOR THE CRUNCHY PEANUT BUTTER
4 ounces (120 g) organic peanuts
1 tbsp. neutral vegetable oil
1 tsp. honey

FOR THE BLACK SESAME WHIPPED CREAM
10 tbsp. (15 cl) of 30 %
M.F. cream, very cold
1 tbsp. and 1 tsp. (10 g)
of powdered sugar
1 tbsp. black sesame paste
1 level tsp.
of powdered charcoal

EQUIPMENT

Mixer
Electric mixer
Piping bag

You never know what to expect with Mikey Sano, he is capable of anything! One thing you can be sure of is that he loves dorayaki. Here is a surprising version for a new take on the classic recipe!

✤ First, prepare the dorayaki batter. Break the eggs into a mixing bowl. Add the sugar and honey and mix vigorously with a whisk. Add the flour, baking powder and baking soda. Mix until smooth. Stir in the oil. Plastic wrap (clingfilm) and place in the refrigerator for 15 minutes.

✤ In the meantime, make the crunchy peanut butter. Heat a pan over medium heat and roast 3 ½ ounces (100 g) of peanuts for 1 to 2 min before putting them in a blender. Blend them in several stages: first 30 seconds to reduce them to a powder, then 4 to 5 minutes. You will see their consistency change from powder to thick and lumpy and finally to almost smooth. Crush and add the remaining peanuts (20 g), oil, and honey and mix with a wooden spoon. Set aside.

✤ Next, prepare the whipped cream: pour the whipping cream into a mixing bowl and whip vigorously (with a hand whisk or electric whisk) until it thickens. Add the powdered sugar, black sesame paste, and charcoal. Whisk vigorously for 1 more minute. Put the whipped cream into a piping bag and refrigerate until ready to serve.

✤ Heat a frying pan over medium heat and, using a paper towel, brush it with oil. Using a ladle, pour the dorayaki mixture into the pan to make small discs. When you see bubbles appear on the surface of the dough, you can turn it over and let it cook for another 1 to 2 minutes. Make an even number of small discs. Let them cool for a few minutes before garnishing them.

✤ Place 1 heaped teaspoon of crunchy peanut butter on the surface of a disk, then add a generous amount of sesame whipped cream on top. Cover with another disk. Repeat until all ingredients are used up.

✤ Enjoy the dorayaki immediately!

Note: in the anime and the manga, Mikey eats a dorayaki with anko paste. Here, I wanted to propose something with a different flavor, but similar look. If you want to recreate Mikey's version more authentically, you can find my recipe for homemade anko in Tips (see page 116).

FULLMETAL
ALCHEMIST

LEVEL ✦ ✦
For 4 people
Preparation time: 30 min
Cooking time: 40 min

WINRY APPLE PIE

BRAIDED APPLE AND RHUBARB PIE

INGREDIENTS

14 ounces (400 g) homemade
shortcrust pastry (see Tip page 116)
or store-bought shortcrust pastry
1 ¾ tbsp. (25 g) butter
5 cups (750 g) apples
The juice of 1 lemon
1 ½ cups (250 g) rhubarb
1 level tsp. cinnamon powder
½ cup (50 g) powdered sugar
2 tbsp. honey
1 ¾ tbsp. (25 g) butter
1 egg yolk
A few pinches of brown sugar

There are many dishes that Alphonse can't wait to devour once he's back in his real body: one of them is definitely the apple pie recipe that Gracia Hughes taught Winry!

❖ Preheat the oven to 392°F (200°C / gas mark 6).

❖ Start by preparing the dough: roll it out to a thickness of 3 mm. Then cut it into 2 discs; place one on a sheet of parchment paper and place it in the refrigerator. Line a heavy pie tin with the second disk. With the tip of a fork, prick the bottom of the pastry all over and place it in the refrigerator while you prepare the apple-rhubarb filling.

❖ Begin the filling by preparing the fruit; peel the apples, remove their cores, and cut them into cubes. Place them in a large bowl and sprinkle with lemon juice. Peel the rhubarb, cut it into cubes and add it to the apples.

❖ Add the cinnamon, sugar, and honey. Using a wooden spoon, mix everything together until it is well-blended. Set aside for a few moments.

❖ Melt the butter in a saucepan over low heat or in the microwave. Pour the butter over the fruit mixture and mix well. Set aside for a few moments.

❖ Remove the pie tin from the refrigerator and insert the fruit mixture. Then, cover the whole thing with the disc of dough that had been cooling in the fridge. If you want to make braids or plaits out of the dough, now is the time!

❖ All that's left to do is finish off the pie: using a brush, brush the pie with the egg yolk. Gently sprinkle with brown sugar and bake for 20 minutes. Lower the temperature to 356°F (180 °C / gas mark 4) and bake for another 15 minutes, keeping an eye on the pastry to make sure it doesn't blacken (you can also cover the pie with a sheet of aluminum foil).

Serve hot and enjoy! Well, now that's done, who fancies one of Gracia Hughes's vegetable quiches?

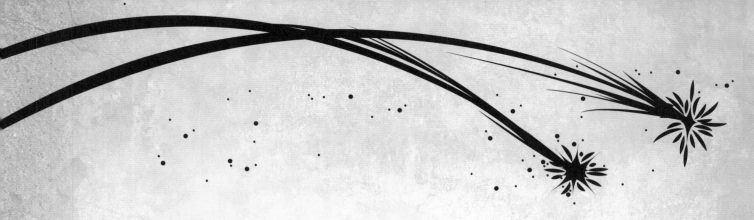

DREAM PANCAKES

PUFFED PANCAKES, MELON, BLUEBERRIES, MAPLE SYRUP

YOUR NAME

LEVEL ✦
For 4 people
Preparation time: 30 min
Cooking time: 10 min

INGREDIENTS

½ melon
2 slices of pineapple
3 ½ ounces (100 g) fresh
blueberries
8 raspberries
Maple syrup
Powdered sugar
Butter

FOR THE PANCAKE MIX
4 egg yolks
6 egg whites
3 tbsp. and 1 tsp. (50 ml)
whole milk
2 tbsp. vegetable oil
1 tsp. vanilla extract
½ cup (60 g) wheat flour type T45
1 pinch of salt
½ cup (80 g) sugar

EQUIPMENT

Electric mixer
Piping bag

If you were ever transported into someone else's body in Tokyo, far from your lakeside village, you would probably want to discover as many things as possible: the pastries of a Tokyo café are probably one of them! Here's what you need to prepare Tokyo's dreamiest pancakes!

❖ Start by preparing the fruit that will be used to top your delicious pancakes. Peel the melon and pineapple and cut them into irregular pieces. Set them aside.

❖ Move on to preparing the pancake mix: pour the egg yolks into a mixing bowl. Add the whole milk, oil, and vanilla extract. Mix well with a whisk for 4 to 5 minutes until a film begins to form. Sift in the flour and whisk it in. Set aside for a few moments.

❖ To make the mix as light and airy as a soufflé, the trick is to beat the egg whites and work them into a French meringue, squeezing them with sugar. For this, pour the egg whites into a bowl, add the salt and, using an electric mixer, beat them until they are stiff. Add the sugar in 3 batches and beat until you have a silky, shiny, pearly texture. Whip until the mixture begins to peak at the top like a bird's beak. Your meringue is ready!

❖ Take 1 tablespoon of meringue and add it to the previous pancake mixture. Then, with a whisk and gently, without breaking it, incorporate the remaining meringue in 3 batches to the pancake mixture. Put the mix into the piping bag.

❖ Brush a skillet with vegetable oil and place over low heat. Pipe a generous amount of pancake mix into the pan. Repeat the process 3 times and cover the pan. You should have enough for 2 pancakes per person. Cook on low heat for 3 to 4 minutes on each side. Serve and enjoy immediately, as soufflés don't like to wait!

To serve, place 2 pancakes on each plate. Add 1 knob of butter to each hot pancake and sprinkle with powdered sugar. Spread the fruit on each plate and pour a delicate drizzle of maple syrup. Enjoy! These pancakes also go great with a caramel latte.

CASE CLOSED

LEVEL ✦ ✦
For 4 people
Preparation time: 30 min
Rest time: 2 h
Cooking time: 40 min

RAN'S DOUBLE CRUST LEMON PIE

CREAMY YUZU PIE

INGREDIENTS

FOR THE DOUGH
4 cups (500 g) flour + some for the
work surface and mold
1 ¼ cups (150 g) of powdered sugar
1 organic lime (the zest)
1 cup (250 g) of butter
2 egg yolks
1 cup (250 g) very cold water
1 egg (to glaze the dough)

FOR THE YUZU CREAM
1 egg + 2 yolks
½ cup (100 g) of brown sugar
½ cup (50 g) flour
2 cups (500 ml) of whole milk
3 tbsp. yuzu juice (or lemon juice)
1 yuzu or 1 organic lemon (the zest)

What wouldn't you do to make your detective happy? Here's how to make Shinichi Kudo's favorite dessert, lemon pie!

✤ First, prepare the dough. Pour the flour and powdered sugar into a bowl. Add the lime zest. Dice the butter and add it to bowl. Knead the mixture with your fingertips to incorporate the butter until the mixture becomes sandy in texture. Add the cold water and form a smooth ball. Plastic wrap (clingfilm) it and place it in the refrigerator for at least 2 hours.

✤ In the meantime, you can prepare the yuzu cream. Pour the egg and yolks into a mixing bowl. Add the brown sugar and whisk the eggs. Gradually add the flour.

✤ Pour 2 tbsp. of water into a saucepan and add the whole milk. Bring it to a gentle boil. Pour half of the boiling milk into the bowl and whisk in. Pour the contents of the bowl back into the remaining milk and return to a low heat. Allow to thicken while stirring continuously with a wooden spoon, over a very low heat. Once the cream is thick, remove from heat and add the juice and zest of the yuzu or lemon. Your yuzu cream is ready!

✤ Preheat the oven to 356°F (180 °C / gas mark 4). Take your dough and place it on a floured work surface. Using a knife, cut it into 2 equal pieces. Roll them out into 2 equal disks.

✤ Flour and line a pie pan with one of the dough disks. Top with the yuzu cream. Cover with the second disk of dough and seal the two disks of dough together. Whip the egg and use it to brown the dough. Make a few openings to let the steam out while cooking and bake for 30 to 40 minutes.

✤ Remove the pie from the oven and let it cool to room temperature before serving! Itadakimasu!

DR STONE

LEVEL ✦
For 4 people
Preparation time: 10 min
Cooking time: 15 min

INGREDIENTS

⅔ inch (2 cm) of fresh ginger
½ bunch fresh cilantro
2 limes
½ cup and 5 tbsp. (200 ml)
liquid honey
1 tbsp. molasses
4 cups (1 l) lemonade or tonic
or cold sparkling water

SENKU COLA

HONEY, CILANTRO, AND LIME SODA

Since your decriminalization, you have been earning the respect of your companions through your scientific knowledge and inventions. The formula for this miracle fluid is one of them. It's as inventive as coca cola in the stone age!

✤ Start by preparing the fresh ginger: peel it and slice it very thinly with a paring knife. Rinse the fresh coriander. Set aside. Zest the limes, reserve the zest, and squeeze the lemons.

✤ Pour the liquid honey, molasses, zest, and juice of the limes into a saucepan. Mix and heat over medium heat for 5 minutes. Add the ginger and fresh coriander. Bring to a boil, then reduce heat to low. Continue to cook over low heat for 10 minutes.

✤ Strain the preparation and you have a concentrated cola syrup! You can keep it for 1 week in the refrigerator.

✤ Now you can make your own senku cola. Pour 1 tbsp. of syrup into each glass and top it off with your choice of lemonade, tonic, or soda water. And there you go!

TIPS

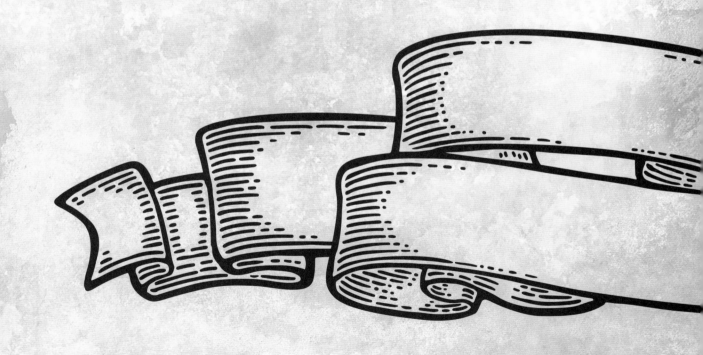

DASHI BROTH WITH DRIED BONITO (KATSUOBUSHI DASHI)

Preparation time: 5 min
Cooking time: 15 min
Rest time: 15 min

INGREDIENTS
8 cups (2 l) spring water
(or tap water)
⅓ ounce (10 g) kombu seaweed
6 tbsp. (40 g) katsuobushi
(grated dried bonito)

• Place the seaweed pieces in a large saucepan and add water. Bring to a simmer and add the bonito. Bring back to a simmer and remove the pan from the heat.

• Cover and let stand for 35 minutes, then strain the mixture. Your dashi is ready!

VEGAN DASHI BROTH

Preparation time: 5 min.
Cooking time: 15 min.

INGREDIENTS
8 cups (2 l) spring water
(or tap water)
⅓ ounce (10 g) kombu seaweed
4 dried shiitakes
1 tbsp. of vegan soy sauce

• Place the seaweed and the dried mushrooms in a large saucepan, add the water and the soy sauce. Bring to a simmer and remove from heat.

• Cover and let stand for 35 minutes, then strain. It's ready!

BEEF BROTH

Preparation time: 10 min
Rest time: 1 h
Cooking time: 4 h 30

INGREDIENTS
2 lbs. and 3 ounces (1 kg) beef chunks
8 cups (2 l) sparkling water
12 and ½ cups (3 l) spring water (or tap water)
1 large onion
2 carrots
1 leek
2 dried shiitakes
1 bouquet garni (bundle of herbs tied with a string)
1 clove
1 ½ tbsp. (25 g) of coarse salt
A few peppercorns
Grape seed oil
Salt

• Start to prepare the meat 1 hour before cooking: cut it into small cubes and keep the bones. Place the meat in a bowl and cover with sparkling water: it will collect some of the blood and impurities of the meat. Keep aside in the refrigerator.

• Now prepare the aromatic garnish. Peel the onion and carrots. Cut them into mirepoix-sized pieces. Rinse and dry the leek, remove its any stale parts and cut the rest into slices, both the green parts and the white. Set aside.

• In a cast iron casserole, pour 3 tbsp. of grape seed oil and heat over medium heat. Place the vegetables in the casserole and brown them for 5 minutes, stirring regularly. Once the aromatic garnish is cooked, remove it for a few moments.

• Place the casserole over high heat. Drain and dry the meat, then salt it finely on all sides and place the beef cubes and trimmings in the casserole. Brown everything well for 10 minutes, stirring with a wooden spoon, then add the aromatic garnish. Add the mushrooms and the bouquet garni, as well as the clove, the coarse salt, and the pepper. Immediately deglaze with plain water and use a wooden spatula to remove the juices from the bottom of the pot.

• Bring to a simmer. Continue cooking at low temperature for 4 hours while skimming regularly to remove impurities.

• At the end of the cooking time, strain the contents of the casserole through a cheesecloth to recover the essence. Your beef broth is ready!

Tip: To make an ice cream or demi-glace, reduce the broth while continuing to cook on high heat. Don't hesitate to transfer the contents of your pot into smaller and smaller pans as the broth reduces, in order to promote reduction by concentration.

WHITE POULTRY STOCK

Preparation time: 20 min.
Cooking time: 4 h 15

INGREDIENTS
4 and ½ pounds (2 kg) poultry or rabbit carcass
1 clove of garlic
2 shallots
2 l of water
1 bouquet garni (thyme and bay leaf in a green leek leaf)
1 sprig of rosemary
2 juniper berries
1 pinch of cracked pepper
6 tbsp. and 2 tsp. (100 ml) grape seed oil
3 ¾ tbsp. (50 g) soft butter

• Crush the carcass and brown it in a stewpot with the grape seed oil and butter. Stir and simmer over medium heat until the carcass turns blonde. Remove and set aside.

• Preheat the oven to 302°F (150°C / gas mark 2). Remove the fat with a small skimmer, keeping the juices at the bottom. Stew the garlic and the chopped shallots in these juices for about 5 minutes on medium heat. Remove from heat.

• Pour the water and add the bouquet garni before cooking the oven for 4 hours, 30 min before the end of the cooking time, add the rosemary, the juniper, and the crushed pepper, and put it back in the oven.

• This infusion will bring a strong taste to your stock, let the herbs and spices infuse. At the end of the 4 hours of cooking, strain the contents of the stewpot to keep only the juice.

VEGETABLE BROTH

Preparation time: 5 min
Cooking time: 2 h
Rest time: 30 min

INGREDIENTS

4 carrots
1 white leek
½ stalk of celery
1 onion

1 bouquet garni
(1 green leek, 4 stalks
of parsley, 1 stalk of
fennel, 1 bay leaf,
1 stalk of thyme)
1 shallot

8 cups (2 l) water
½ cup and 2 tbsp.
(150 ml) white wine
1 star anise
3 cardamoms

- Dice the carrots. Cut the leek, celery, and onion into small pieces.

- Put all the ingredients in a pot and simmer for 2 hours covered.

- Let it rest for 30 minutes off the heat, then strain the broth.

FISH BROTH (FISH STOCK)

Preparation time: 20 min
Cooking time: 40 min

INGREDIENTS

2 onions
2 leeks
1 celery stalk
14 ounces (400 g) fish trimmings
and bones (ask your fishmonger)
6 tbsp. and 2 tsp. (100 ml) mirin
4 cups (1 l) water
1 bouquet garni
3 ¾ tbsp. (50 g) soft butter
Grape seed oil

- Peel the onions and chop them finely. Rinse the leeks and celery and cut them into small cubes.

- In a casserole dish, heat a drop of olive oil and butter over medium heat. Once the butter has melted, add the fish trimmings and bones. Sauté for 1 minute and then add the shallots, onions, leeks, and celery. Fry for another minute before adding the mirin. Mix well and add water to the top. Add the bouquet garni, cover and cook over low heat for 35 minutes. Skim regularly.

- At the end of the cooking time, strain the contents of the pot to keep only the clear juice of the fish stock.

- Tip: You can use this delicious broth for cooking or as a sauce to accompany seafood dishes.

HOMEMADE KETCHUP

For 1 small bottle
Preparation time: 10 min.
Cooking time: 30 min.

INGREDIENTS

1 clove of garlic
1 red onion
6 ripe tomatoes
2 pinches of ground cumin
2 pinches of ground ginger
2 tbsp. tomato paste
1 ½ tbsp. (20 g) brown sugar
6 tbsp. and 2 tsp. (100 ml) red wine vinegar
2 tbsp. olive oil
Salt and pepper

• First prepare the vegetables: peel the garlic and onion. Chop them finely and set them aside. Peel the tomatoes and cut them into large pieces. Set them aside.

• In a saucepan, heat the olive oil over medium heat. Add the garlic and onion and sauté for 3 minutes. Sprinkle with cumin and ground ginger and stir in the tomato paste. Using a wooden spoon, mix well and add the crushed tomatoes. Mix and add brown sugar. Bring to a boil, then simmer over low heat, covered, for 15 minutes, then uncovered for an additional 10 minutes, so that the mixture softens. Add the wine vinegar and season with salt and pepper.

• Using a hand blender, blend the mixture for 2 minutes and pass it through a sieve. Let it cool before bottling.

JAPANESE MAYONNAISE

For 10 tbsp. (15 cl)
Preparation time: 2 min

INGREDIENTS

4 tbsp. ketchup	1 tbsp. mustard
2 tbsp.	1 pinch of salt
Worcestershire sauce	1 tsp. sugar
1 tbsp.	1 tsp. rice (or cider)
soy sauce	vinegar 1 tbsp. lemon
1 tsp. mirin	(or yuzu) juice 6 tbsp.
1 tsp.	(5 ml) neutral vegetable
1 tsp. honey	oil (rapeseed, sunflower
1 egg yolk	or grape seed)

• Start by pouring the egg yolk, mustard, sugar and salt into a bowl. Mix well, then add the vinegar and lemon juice.

• Whilst whisking, add the oil, pouring it in little by little. Emulsify until you have a smooth and creamy mixture!

OKONOMI SAUCE

For 6 tbsp. and
2 tsp. (100 ml)
Preparation time:
2 min

INGREDIENTS

4 tbsp. ketchup
2 tbsp. Worcestershire sauce
1 tbsp. soy sauce
1 tsp. mirin
1 tsp. honey

In a bowl, mix all the ingredients until you get a thick and smooth sauce!

BURGER BUN

Preparation time: 15 min
Rest time: 1 h 15
Cooking time: 20 min

INGREDIENTS
3 cups (340 g) flour type T55
1 packet of baking powder
1 ½ tsp. (6 g) sugar
1 tsp. (6 g) salt
½ cup and 5 tbsp. (200 ml) warm milk
4 tbsp. (55 g) butter or 1 egg yolk

• Place and mix the flour, yeast, salt, and sugar in a bowl. Add the warm milk. Knead with your fingertips to obtain a smooth mixture.

• Place the mixture in the bowl of a food processor and pulse on low speed for 2 to 3 minutes. Add the butter to the bowl of a food processor and pulse for an additional 7 minutes, until the dough is smooth and shiny.

• Cover the dough with a tea towel and let it rise for 45 minutes.

• Flour your work surface: place the dough on it and degas it. Separate the dough into 4 equal pieces.

• Shape them by folding the dough inwards. Repeat until you have smooth balls. Flour them and your hands, if necessary, to make them easier to handle. Cover them again and let them rise for another 30 minutes.

• Brush them with egg yolk before baking for 20 min.

KONJAC

Konjac is a tuber that has been used in Japanese cooking and medicine for hundreds of years. It is used to make noodles or vermicelli (shirataki) which can be found quite easily in Asian grocery stores. Konjac is prized for its medicinal virtues but also because it does not contain gluten and is therefore suitable for people with gluten intolerance.

STENCIL

ULTRA-SPICY BURGER

SHORTCRUST PASTRY

For 1 ½ cup (250 g) dough
Preparation time: 10 min
Rest time: 2 h

INGREDIENTS
1 ¾ cups (250 g) flour
½ cup (125 g) cold butter
½ cup (125 g) very cold water
1 ¼ tsp. (5 g) salt

- Put the flour and salt in a bowl. Mix well and add the butter in pieces. Knead the mixture for 2 minutes by hand and then sand the mixture between your fingers.

- Pour in the ice water at once to create a thermal shock and knead again for 1 min, until a smooth ball of pastry is formed.

- Cover with plastic wrap (clingfilm) and place in the refrigerator for 2 hours.
- Your shortcrust pastry is ready to use.

ANKO BATTER

For 2 cups (350 g) dough
Preparation time: 10 min
Rest time: 2 h
Cooking time: 1 h 15

INGREDIENTS
7 ounces (200 g) azuki beans
3 cups (70 cl) mineral water
1 cup (180 g) sugar
1 pinch of salt

- Soak the azuki beans for 2 hours in a container of cold water.

- Drain and place in a saucepan. Cover them with water and bring to a boil. Let it simmer for 5 minutes. Drain the beans and repeat the process, changing the water.

- Once the beans are blanched and bitter-free, pour the mineral water into the pot and immerse the beans. Cook them at a low boil for 50 minutes to 1 hour, until they are melting in the middle.

- Remove from heat and leave in the water for an additional 10 minutes.

- Remove a third of the cooking water, add the sugar and a pinch of salt. Over medium heat, resume cooking and simmer for another 15 to 20 minutes, stirring regularly. The idea is to let the preparation reduce to a nice purée, not too liquid but slightly syrupy. Your batter is ready!

measurements

OVEN TEMPERATURES

Gas Mark 1	=	275°F	=	135 °C
Gas Mark 2	=	300°F	=	149 °C
Gas Mark 3	=	325°F	=	163 °C
Gas Mark 4	=	350°F	=	177 °C
Gas Mark 5	=	375°F	=	191 °C
Gas Mark 6	=	400°F	=	204 °C
Gas Mark 7	=	425°F	=	218 °C
Gas Mark 8	=	450°F	=	232 °C

VOLUME / WEIGHT

1 ML = 1 G

1 CL = 10 G

1 DL = 100 G

1 L = 1 000 G

SPOON / SIZES

INGREDIENT		TEASPOON		TABLESPOON
Powdered sugar	=	5 g	=	15 g
Flour, semolina	=	4 g	=	12 g
Butter	=	5 g	=	15 g
Fresh cream	=	5 ml	=	15 ml
Oil	=	5 ml	=	15 ml
Salt	=	5 g	=	15 g
Pepper	=	2 g	=	5 g

Acknowledgements

If you've made it this far, you know that it's time to say thank-you to everyone who helped make this book happen!

Thank you Bérengère for this new collaboration, for your artistic direction and for the passion that you put into our projects year after year!

Henri, you will discover some of these cult references with time, I can't wait to share this with you and to discover with you the mangas and anime that will inspire your dreams!

Thanks to my parents and my sister for their unfailing support, love and trust. I will always remember the first manga I bought with my father at the newspaper stand in Châtillon. I was 8 years old and it was volume 4 of *Dragon Ball*, the pastel version. I still have it at home. Thank you, dad, for your open-mindedness.

Thanks to Nicolas, whose brilliant eye and professionalism I can always count on!

Thank you Mehdiya, for your work, your passion and your commitment!

Thank you to my team, and especially to Baptiste, my trusted right-hand man who allows me to create in freedom and peace.

Thank you to all the people who helped me with this book, with their advice, their gifts, their time. A special thanks to my dear Marie and to Ken for their advice concerning the book's many references.

Thank you, Olivier, you publishing veteran. You don't realize it, but your look at pop culture and your vision of these universes never gets old and are an example I try to follow every day.

Thanks to Catherine and Antoine from Hachette Heroes, for another successful collaboration to be proud of!

Anne, thank you for being such an understanding, open, and passionate editor. Thank you for your patience with me, I know I'm not easy to work with sometimes. Yes, I've written these words before, but you're still as professional as ever and I'm still as complicated to work with. I'm just happy that we manage to create books that are always so great!

Thank you to all the team at Hachette Heroes who will bring this book to you, the public, and give it the spotlight it deserves.

A final and big thank you to my dear community, readers, viewers, fans of the dawn or spectators of the shade. Thank you. Thank you. Thank you.

Thibaud Villanova

Director: Catherine Saunier-Talec
Project Director: Antoine Béon
Project manager: Anne Vallet
Design and illustrations: Bérengère Demoncy
Correction: Charlotte Buch-Müller
Production: Anne-Laure Soyez

Illustrations: Bérengère Demoncu, except for the illustrations on pages 12, 41 (Benoît Simonpietri), and pages 31, 99 (Adobe Stock: PikePicture, alvaroc)

Photo styling: Mehdiya Kerairia, except for the photos on pages 32-33, 35, 68-69, 103, 104, 107 (Séverine Augé), and pages 36, 80, 84-85, 87, 89, 97, 100 (Soizic Chomel de Varagnes).

Image credits:
Adobe stock: Julietphotography, oxinoxi, valterz, artrise
Printed in China by Toppan Leefung
WWW.GASTRONOGEEK.COM

Titan
BOOKS

A division of Titan Publishing Group Ltd 144 Southwark Street London SE1 0UP www.titanbooks.com
Find us on Facebook: www.facebook.com/titanbooks Follow us on Twitter: @TitanBooks
Published by arrangement with Hachette Heroes: www.hachetteheroes.com
A CIP catalogue record for this title is available from the British Library

ISBN: 9781803366289